THE MAHABHARATA

THE MAHABHARATA

A CRITICISM

C.V. VAIDYA M.A., LL.B.

GYAN

Published by

GYAN

Gyan Publishing House
5, Ansari Road
Daryaganj, New Delhi-110002
Phone: 011-47034999, 9811692060
E-mail: books@gyanbooks.com

Distribution Network
gyanbooks.com
India, USA, Canada, UK, Australia, France

ISBN : 978-81-212-9681-6 (PB)
First Published, 1905

2nd Impression 2023

Printed at: Gyan Press, Delhi.

THE MAHABHARATA : A CRITICISM
Author: C.V. VAIDYA

THE MAHABHARATA: A CRITICISM.

BY

Ç. V. VAIDYA, M.A., LL.B.,

Honorary Fellow of the University of Bombay.

1905

CONTENTS.

I—THE MAHABHARATA AS A POEM

—THE MAHABHARATA AS A HISTORY

APPENDIX.

PREFACE.

A CRITICAL study of the Mahabharata and the Ramayana, in conjunction with other works bearing on the subject, has suggested to me several new ideas about them which I propose to place before the public in three instalments. The present volume contains my views on the Mahabharata, considered from the literary and historical stand-points. If the views published in this volume impress the public favourably, I may be encouraged to publish a second volume giving my views on the Ramayana from the same stand-points. In a third volume I intend to take a survey of the social, religious and intellectual conditions of the Aryans of India between 3000 and 300 B.C. as evidenced by these venerable epics.

"Sankshipta Mahabharata" or "Mahabharata abridged," a book recently published by me, if read along with this book, will be found to contain most of the original Shlokas of the Mahabharata on which this criticism is based.

Owing to the haste with which this book was carried through the press, some errors of spelling have crept in, especially with regard to Sanskrit words, the spelling of which does not often conform to the now generally adopted rules of writing Sanskrit words in English characters. I hope the indulgent reader will overlook such inaccuracies.

It is just possible that some of my readers may have facts or arguments to advance against the views propounded in this book—views which at present seem to be unshakeable. If therefore any of my readers wish to communicate with me in addition to, or instead of, criticising the work in the press, such communications should be addressed to me, to the care of Mr. Yande, Manager of the *Induprakash* Press, to whom my thanks are due for the interest he took in the publication of this volume.

C. V. VAIDYA.

BOMBAY, *December* 1904.

INSCRIBED WITH PERMISSION

TO

His Highness The Maharaja Sayajirao

Gaekwar of Baroda,

SENAKHASKHEL SAMSHER BAHADUR,

G.C.S.I.,

IN RESPECTFUL ADMIRATION OF HIS HIGHNESS'S

SINCERE LOVE AND GENEROUS PATRONAGE

OF LEARNING.

THE MAHABHARATA AS A POEM.

ERRATA

INE				
30	*for*	this	*read*	his
9	,,	cries	,,	creed
20	,,	is	,,	was
21	,,	semin	,	semen
25	,,	Magesthene	,,	Megasthenes
11	,,	,,	,,	,,
14	,,	point	,,	points
6	,	instances	,,	incidents
3	,,	discussed	,,	dismissed
6	,,	praise	,,	praises

THE MAHABHARATA AS A POEM.

CHAPTER I.

The Three Editions of the Work.

THAT the Mahabharata in its present form is the second amplification of an orginally much smaller work, nobody can consistently deny. We have the authority of the Mahabharata itself for the statement that Vyasa, the author of the original work, taught it to five pupils, one of whom was Vaishampayana. Vaishampayana recited the poem before king Janmejaya at the time of the Sarpa-satra (serpent sacrifice), performed by him. Now in the Mahabharata, as we have it, there are several questions asked by Janmejaya, and Vaishampayana gives suitable answers. How can these questions and answers have formed part of the original epic composed by Vyasa ? We must hold that Vaishampayana, or some one who heard the recitation and the dialogue, amplified the original work. Then, again, this amplified Bharata was recited by Sauti before Shaunaka at his twelve years' sacrifice, and certain questions are asked by Shaunaka and answered by Sauti. These cannot have formed part either of the original work or the amplified edition of Vaishampayana. We are, therefore, compelled to admit that Sauti, or some one else who heard his recitation, amplified the original work a second time.

These three editions, if we may so call them, can further be proved by various other statements still preserved in the Mahabharata itself, either by oversight or owing to absence of motive to expunge them We have thus the statement that the work is supposed to have three beginnings Some believe, it said, that the Mahabharata begins with Uparichara, others with Astika, and others still with the word Manu [1] Different lengths are also assigned to the work, and different divisions are also mentioned, and even different names can be easily discovered We shall see how these different names, divisions and lengths can well be explained on the theory that there were two amplifications of the original work

The Original Work —The original epic was probably in its nature a history and not a didactic work It is specially called an Itihasa or history, and the name which Vyasa gave to this history was Jaya or "Triumph" [2] The very first invocation verse contains a mention of this name "Tato jayamudirayet" We have the same name again given to the work in the last Parva also The length of this historical poem of Vyasa cannot be ascertained with any exactness, though it is probable that it must have been a long one even then, considering the ambitious scheme of the author, the importance and the grandeur of the events described, and the facility with which Anushtub shlokas can be composed by a gifted author MacDonell remarks

[1] Manvadi Bharatam kechidastikadi tathapare
Tathoparicharadyanye viprah samyagadhiyate—Adi 1 52

Jayo nametihasoyam —Swargarohana Parva

that the length of the original poem of Vyasa is mentioned as 8,800 shlokas. This is in our opinion not true, and for this remark, perhaps, a foot-note in Weber[1] is responsible. This figure[2] is given in the Mahabharata, as the number of Kuta shlokas or riddles, of which we shall have to speak hereafter, and not as the number of shlokas in the original Mahabharata itself. It is mentioned in the Mahabharata that the industrious Krishnadwaipayana or Vyasa composed his poem in three years, working day and night. It would be natural to expect that Vyasa would begin his work with an account of himself, and the idea that Bharata really begins with Uparichara seems very justifiable indeed. In the chapter preceding the 63rd Chapter which begins with "Rajoparicharo nama," a praise of the Mahabharata and some facts about its composition are given by Vaishampayana which clearly shows that these 62 chapters in the Adi Parva are later additions made by either Vaishampayana or Sauti. This does not mean that the work subsequent to Chapter 62 is in the words of Vyasa himself. For, it seems probable that the whole has been so overhauled that it is impossible now to point to any portion of the succeeding work as the composition of the original author himself.

The Second Edition.—We now come to the second edition, *viz.*, the edition of Vaishampayana, who, as has been stated before, was Vyasa's own pupil and was

[1] Foot-note 206, Weber, page 187. The same statement is given by Mr. Dutt.

[2] Ashtau shloka sahasrani ashtau shloka shatanicha
Aham vedmi shuko vetti Sanjayo vetti va na va.—Adi. 81-3.

taught the Bharata along with four others, *viz.*, Sumantu, Jaimini, Paila and Shuka, the son of Vyasa. There is a statement in the Bharata itself that each one of these five pupils published a different edition of the Bharata. This is an express authority for us to hold that Vaishampayana almost recast the whole, and brought out his own version. That version is the only one now preserved to us, though we have one doubtful Ashwamedha Parva under the name of Jaimini. It seems, however, probable that five different versions were really extant in the days of Ashwalayana who has enumerated all these five Rishis as Bharatacharyas or the editors of Bharata. This also shows that Vaishampayana and his co-pupils' works first came to be called Bharata. The extent of Vaishampayana's Bharata appears to have been 24,000 verses; for, there is a shloka in the Mahabharata that Vyasa composed Bharata Samhita (this word is important) of that extent, and that work without its Upakhyanas is called Bharata. In this Bharata there was a summary chapter at the beginning, covering 150 shlokas, in which the number of chapters and the Parvas were also mentioned. Vaishampayana would naturally begin his version with an account of Janmejaya, and his Sarpasatra, where he recited his poem, and thus we have the second beginning assigned to the Mahabharata, *viz.*, with the Astikopakhyana.

The Third Edition.—We lastly come to the third edition of Sauti. That Sauti did recast or elaborate the work of Vaishampayana can be proved from his own lips. "Know ye, Rishis," says he, "I have recited the Bharata in one hundred thousand shlokas;

Vaishampayana being the first reciter in this human world."[1] This is a clear admission by Sauti of having recited the work of Vaishampayana in one lac of shlokas.

The chapters which precede the Astika story cannot have formed part of Vaishampayana's book, and thus we have the third beginning assigned to the Mahabharata, *viz.*, with the word Manu,[2] as properly applicable to Sauti's edition. This edition has come down to us nearly in the form which Sauti gave to it. For anticipating the modern idea of an edition, Sauti has added to his work a preface, an introduction and a table of contents. It thus assumed almost a fixed form. The present Mahabharata, in fact, contains about a thousand less shlokas than the number given by Sauti (96,836, *see* Appendix No. 1), though additional shlokas and chapters are found here and there. The commentator generally notices the excess, if any, at the end of a Parva, and strangely enough, ascribes it to the mistake of writers. Such shlokas and chapters in excess are chiefly to be found in the Adi and the Drona Parvas.[3]

In addition to the preface in which Sauti gives the occasion when, and the place where this recast Mahabharata was recited, Sauti gives us an introduction, giving a summary, as it were, of the long story by the mouth of Dhritarashtra. The 69 shlokas, all beginning

[1] Asminstu manushe loke Vaishampayana uktavan
Ekam shatasahasraṃtu mayoktam vai nibodhata.—Adi. 1-107.

[2] There is no shloka beginning with Manu in the Adi Parva, but the commentator takes it as identical with Vaivaswat.—Adi. 1.

[3] For instance, at the end of Adi Parva the commentator says that there are 237 chapters in the Parva instead of 227, mentioned by Vyasa.

with "Yadashrausham," to be found in the first chapter, cannot have formed part of the original introduction, and being in long metre, are evidently an addition made by Sauti. This is, however, a very ingenious way of summarising a story from the mouth of one of the actors themselves. There was a short summary of the Bharata given by Vaishampayana, as has already been remarked, but that chapter was only in 150 shlokas, while the present chapter exceeds by many shlokas, and this is a further proof of the whole chapter having nearly been recast by Sauti.

Sauti probably gave the work the name of Mahabharata first. Bharata and Mahabharata are names separately mentioned by Ashwalayana, and we are not stretching our guess too far when we assign the name of Bharata to the work of Vaishampayana, and appropriate the latter name to Sauti's voluminous edition. For, Sauti himself has said that the name Mahabharata was given to the work owing to its greatness and its weight.[1] Weber again has pointed out that the name Mahabharata occurs in Panini, but with an entirely different signification (*viz.*, a great Bharata warrior). As Panini mentions Yudhishthira and other names familiar to the Bharata story, we have another proof in support of the idea that the name Mahabharata, as applied to the poem, had no existence in the days of Panini.

Sauti adopted a new division for this now bulky poem, and divided it into 18 Parvas. Another division is mentioned in the Mahabharata itself, which has the same name of Parva, though the number is greater.

[1] Mahatvatbharatatvachcha Mahabharatamuchyate.

It is impossible that these two divisions could have been made at one and the same time, and by one and the same author; for, in that case, the greater and smaller divisions would certainly have been called by different names. For example, if a work is divided into books, the sub-divisions of the latter cannot be called by the same name of books, but will have to be styled chapters or sections. We should, at least, expect tha the word "smaller" would be attached to the sub-divisions. This clearly shows that Vaishampayana's work was not divided into 18 Parvas, but into a large number of smaller divisions, which were called Parvas by him. Sauti adopted a larger and more suitable division, but retained the same name of Parva. We have thus sometimes the absurdity of a sub-Parva having the same name as the big Parva, *e.g.*, there is a Sauptika Parva under the big Sauptika Parva, a Sabha Parva under the bigger Sabha Parva. These Parvas are again subdivided into Adhyayas or chapters. Vyasa's original work was presumably divided into Parvas and Adhyayas also, but the number of Parvas was most likely less than 100, the number assigned to Vaishampayana's edition. As usual, we have strong confirmation of this view in the Mahabharata itself. In Chapter II, Adi Parva, where the hundred Parvas are given, we are told that the Harivamsha[1] is a Khila Parva, *i.e.*, a Parva borrowed from another place. The Harivamsha, it follows, did not form part of Vyasa's work, and was brought in by Vaishampayana. No doubt, the story of

[1] Harivamshastatah parva puranam khila samjnitam
Etatparva shatam purnam Vyasenoktam mahatmana.

the Mahabharata war does not look complete without a Parva giving the life and exploits of Shri Krishna, in the same way as the story of the Ramayana would not have been complete without an account of Ravana's life and exploits; and the Harivamsha stands to the Bharata in the same relation as the Uttarkanda stands to the Ramayana. Harivamsha, contrary to the Uttarkanda, however, is usually left out of the Mahabharata, which stands by itself and ends as if nothing is to follow it. The hundred Parvas of Vaishampayana, still retained in the Mahabharata, are given in the appendix. The number of Parvas, as they are enumerated in the Adi Parva, Chapter I, certainly exceeds one hundred, and this is itself sufficient to show that the Bharata of Vaishampayana was amplified by Sauti. These hundred Parvas Sauti put together in 18, as he himself admits. For, he says, "these hundred Parvas" were composed by Vysa, but thereafter Lomaharshani, the son of Suta, recited 18 Parvas only in the Naimisharanya.

To summarise the above, the present Mahabharata is, as it were, a redaction of Vyasa's historical poem called "Triumph" edited by Vaishampayana as Bharata, and reprinted or reissued by Sauti, with notes and additions, and with an introduction and a table of contents prefixed to it. We shall now pass on to discuss whether these reputed authors were real beings.

CHAPTER II.

VYASA, VAISHAMPAYANA AND SAUTI.

THE author of the original epic is generally believed to be Vyasa, whose personality is doubted by many. Now we have already seen that the final redaction was made by Sauti, and not by Vyasa. There is, moreover, no reason why a general tradition should not be believed if it is not absurd or impossible in itself, or is not disproved by contradictory cogent arguments. Vyasa is believed to have arranged the Vedas,[1] and not the Mahabharata. That there was really a Rishi by name Vyasa Parasharya we find from the Black Yajuh Kathaka. What part he took in the events of the Mahabharata, and when he lived, we shall discuss later on. But there is no reason to doubt that he wrote a history of the war between the Kurus and the Panchalas from personal knowledge. The work evidently bears the impress of a narration by one who had an intimate acquaintance with the events it describes. Characters and people are described with a vivacity and truthfulness which can only belong to the evidence of an eye-witness. Names, such as Srinjayas, are often mentioned without any introduction or description, much in the way of a contemporary narrator who is never struck with the necessity of such an introduction or description. It is generally

[1] Vedam vivyasa yasmattu Vyasa ityabhidheeyâte.

admitted that the actors in the Mahabharata strike us as real living beings. This is so, it will be admitted, because there is a nucleus in the poem which is the composition of one who knows, and not of one who imagines. Nay you sometimes come across statements of facts and sentiments which, like fossils not yet obliterated, give a clue to a real by-gone age. In short, we think, that there is ample ground to believe that there was an original author, who wrote from personal knowledge, and that there is no harm in believing that that author was Vyasa Parasharya.

Vaishampayana is represented as a pupil of Vyasa. Looking to the tradition that he recited his poem before Janmejaya, the great-grandson of Arjuna, Vyasa's contemporary, this relation does not seem impossible. That he was a real person may also be granted from the fact that his name is mentioned as an Acharya of Bharata by Ashwalayana. The evidence of language also is very important in this connection. Although the language of the whole Mahabharata strikes us as old, and differs distinctly from classical Sanskrit, within the Mahabharata itself there are certain portions the language of which looks more ancient than that of others. It is deep, sonorous and weighty in its very simplicity. Its grammar and construction are archaic. It strikes us as the language of an adept using a spoken tongue. We may instance the Bhagwat Gita, which, if not the composition of Vyasa, must, at least, be that of Vaishampayana, whose date, from the evidence of language, must not have been very distant from the date of the Upanishadas.

We now come to Sauti, the last reciter of Mahabharata. His personality is not so clear as that of Vishampayana or Vyasa. He is sometimes styled in the Mahabharata itself as Suta only, and not the son of Suta. His name is given as Ugrashrava, the son of Lomaharshana. He is sometimes styled a Puranik, *i.e.*, a reciter of Puranas. Strangely enough, in the Mahabharata there are two places where he is said to have come to Shaunak. In the very beginning of the poem we are told (the first sentence of the Mahabharata in prose) that Sauti Ugrashrava, son of Lomaharshana, came to Shaunak Kulapati while he was engaged in a twelve years' sacrifice. Being asked whence he came, he said he came from the Sarpa-satra (serpent sacrifice) of Janmejaya where he heard various stories from the Mahabharata, composed by Vyasa and related by Vaishampayana, and then he first went to see Kurukshetra or Syamanta Panchaka where the great battle was fought. At the beginning of Chapter IV, Adi Parva, we have the same sentence in prose again, and the story begins as if the previous 3 Adhyayas were not there. Shaunak here does not ask Sauti whence he came, but says "Your father learned the whole Purana formerly. Have you learned the same? If so, tell us the legend of the family of Bhrigus." Hereafter come the words "Suta uwacha, and not Sauti uwacha." This does not make Suta a contemporary of Vaishampayana, but represents him merely as one who has studied the Puranas.

The commentator has seen the absurdity of these two beginnings, *viz.*, of Chapter I and of Chapter IV, and gives the usual explanation based on the supposition of two Sutas belonging to different Kalpas. Perhaps, there were actually two persons who laboured at the recasting of the Mahabharata into its present voluminous form, and they may have been related to each other as father and son. They were Puraniks or persons whose occupation it is to recite the Puranas. The commentator represents them as Brahmins, though the word Suta means a person born of a Brahmana woman from a Kshatriya. Probably the Sutas by caste followed the occupation of learning the Puranas or old stories by heart, and like the Bhatas of the present day rose in the estimation of the people. Sauti and his father were generally helped by their Puranik lore when recasting the Bharata into its present shape. When this recasting took place and with what purpose, we shall presently see.

CHAPTER III.

WHEN AND WHY THE BHARATA WAS RECAST.

WEBER observes: "The first evidence of the existence of an epic with the contents of the Mahabharata comes to us from Rhetor Dion Chrysostom who flourished in the second half of the first century A.D. Since Megasthenes says nothing of this epic, it is not an improbable hypothesis that its origin is to be placed between Megasthenes and Chrysostom." Weber, the only blemish of whose deep and really wonderful research is a kind of bias, has here forgotten that we have not the work of Megasthenes before us. That most valuable book has been lost. It is only from fragments of it quoted by others that we get some information about India as it was in 300 B.C. But even these fragments mention, as observed by Weber himself, a Herackles and a Pandia, who can be identified as Krishna and his sister. It thus appears clear that the Pandava legend was well known even in the days of Megasthenes (we shall return to this topic in the second book). It cannot, therefore, be believed with Weber that the origin of the Mahabharata is to be placed between 300 B.C. and 50 A.D. This is a very short period indeed for its birth as well as for its growth to such an enormous volume. It seems, however, probable that the last recasting of the

Mahabharata by Sauti into its present shape took place between these dates. We have, on the one hand, the direct evidence of Dion Chrysostom that the Mahabharata, with its one lac of verses, was well known even in the south of India in 50 A.D. Various arguments, on the other hand, can be adduced to prove that the Mahabharata in its present shape cannot be placed earlier than 300 B.C. The first and the foremost among them is the fact that the Yavanas are frequently mentioned in the Mahabharata as a very powerful people. The Indians came into contact with the Yavanas or the Greeks, for the first time, in the days of Alexander, and their connection lasted from that time to about the beginning of the Christian Era. They often defeated the Indians in battle, though they were eventually driven out of India. The following shloka (one amongst many) shows how the Mahabharata looked upon the Yavanas admiringly :—

Na shahsaka vashi kartum yam Pandurapi viryavan
Sorjunena vasham nito rajasidyavanadhipah.

"The king of the Yavanas, whom even the powerful Pandu could not subdue, was reduced to subjection by Arjuna."

Again we have the mention of a Nagna Kshapanaka (naked Jain) in the Paushya Akhyana in the Adi Parva. The origin of Jainism is usually believed to have been laid by Mahabira about 500 B.C., *i.e.*, about the same time as Buddhism. The Mahabharata does not directly refer to Buddhism or to any of its votaries. But this is not an argument to put it before Buddhism. Discussions and discourses in the nature of Buddhistic controversies are hinted at in the Mokshadharma section of the Shanti Parva. Buddhism and Jainism had assumed an offensive appearance, and were threatening to be powerful rivals of the orthodox Aryan religion, and it may be assumed that, while no direct mention is made of Buddha or his tenets, the recasting of the Bharata was due to this very growing evil. At that time Brahmin teachers probably thought it necessary to bring together *en masse* all the floating materials, for the preaching of their religion, into one focus, and hence we have the spectacle of a vast didactic work raised on the foundation of the legend of the Bharata war. Here we find the clue to the fact that the Mahabharata is constantly preaching Dharma and the sanctity of its exponents. Dharma and its preachers, the Brahmanas, appear to have been in danger, and adherence to Dharma and obedience to Brahmanas is constantly insisted upon throughout the Mahabharata. This is, in our opinion, the most probable reason why we find an epic, the Baharata of Vaishampayana or Vyasa, turned into a Dharma Grantha, a Smriti as it is believed to be, a vast didactic work embracing all the departments of the Aryan religion and morals as they were in the days of Megasthenes.

It may, perhaps, be urged that the shlokas containing a reference to the Yavanas and the Shakas may have been introduced after 300 B.C. while the rest of the poem may have been reconstructed at an earlier date. If any confirmation, however, of what has been urged above, is needed, the state of society, religion and knowledge, depicted generally in the Mahabharata, corresponds very closely with what has been described about India by Megasthenes. We find the castes almost exclusive; flesh-eating, though still practised, going out of fashion; Shiva and Vishnu-worship fully established. The geographical knowledge of the whole country had been acquired, and the Mahabharata locates the people of India much in the same way in which Greek geographers have located them. Curiously enough, a people who cover themselves with their ears, are mentioned in the Mahabharata, and this absurdity of nature is spoken of and believed in by Megasthenes. Grammar, Logic and Vedanta were already formulated and studied. We shall discuss this subject in detail in a separate book, but it is sufficient here to remark that the present Mahabharata discloses a state of things which cannot have been earlier than the days of Megasthenes.

Astronomy furnishes us with still more definite data in this connection. In fact, the progress in the development of astronomical knowledge, disclosed by the Mahabharata, shows us the different stages through which the work must have passed. We have thus in the Mahabharata the Nakshatras or constellations beginning with Krittikas, a system which must have been introduced thousands of years ago (as we shall show later on) and which reminds us of the time when Vyasa must have composed the original epic. We have again a reference to the time when the winter solstice took place in Dhanishtha, as mentioned in the Vedanga Jyotisha, whose date Dixit calculates on this basis at about 1400 B.C. We have further still a reference to the time when the winter solstice fell in Shravana, and the Nakshatras were counted as beginning with that constellation. This new arrangement is mentioned as having been introduced by Vishwamitra, "who created another world of his own, and made the Nakshatras begin with Shravana," Adi Parva, Chapter 71. The same beginning is referred to in the Ashwamedha Parva, Chapter 44. This must have been the case according to Dixit's calculation about 450 B.C. The receding of the winter solstice is due, as those who are conversant with astronomy are well aware, to the precession of the equinoxes, and furnishes with very reliable data in fixing the limits, if not an actual date. The present Mahabharata thus, which contains a reference to the Shravana beginning of the Nakshatras, cannot be earlier than 450 B.C. (*see* Dixit's History of Indian Astronomy, p. 14).

Dixit's very valuable work called "The History of Indian Astronomy," referred to herein, has unfortunately not yet been translated into English. Dixit's deep researches in this subject, and his conclusions, are generally unbiased and worthy of respectful consideration. In one point, however, he seems to have been misled, and we have to refer to it because it is relevant to the inquiry now before us. It is admitted by all, and by Dixit also, that the Mahabharata, as it is at present, makes no mention whatever of the Rashis (the division of the ecliptic into twelve houses) and of the Varas (week days). Dixit believes that the Rashis were invented by Indian astronomers about 425 B.C. (p. 139, Dixit's work). It seems, however, very probable that Dixit has wrongly assigned this date to this event in order that it may not be possible to contend that the Rashis were borrowed from the Greeks, with whom India came into contact in 323 B.C., for the first time, and whose connection with this country lasted for about three centuries. How far Indian astronomy is indebted to the Greeks, is a subject on which much has been written on both sides. This much cannot, however, be denied that Indian astronomy derived a fresh impetus and received a new direction from its contact with Greek astronomy. All the Siddhantas, which give methods for calculating the exact positions of the planets, date subsequent to 300 B.C., as Dixit himself has admitted. Now these methods are based on the division of the ecliptic into Rashis and degrees, and not on the division of the ecliptic into Nakshatras hitherto prevalent in India. The conclusion is thus very strong that the Rashis must have been borrowed from the Greeks. Dixit in denying this conclusion relies on two arguments chiefly. (P. 515-16.) He says that the Rashis have Sanskrit names, and secondly, that as Aries or Mesha is made to begin with the constellation Ashwini, this connection must have been established, according to his calculation, about 471 B.C. Now Dixit has forgotten to notice the fact that the Sanskrit names of the Rashis are the exact equivalents of their Greek names. The figures (the Ram, the Bull, &c.) which are supposed to be formed by the constellations (Ashwini, &c.) are all imaginary ones, a fact also admitted by Dixit himself. How can it be possible, then, that two nations independently imagined the same figures? The names of the Rashis, though in Sanskrit, to our mind are an argument in favour of their Greek origin rather than against it. Nay, Greek names of the Rashis were known to the Indian astronomers and are often used by them as equivalent of the Sanskrit names. The other argument also is not of any avail. The only thing that it proves, is that the Rashis cannot have been introduced in India earlier than 475 B.C. But they may have been and were actually introduced later. For, no Indian astronomer has taken the first point of Aries as coincident with Batarius, the first star in the Ashwini constellation. On the contrary, the Surya Siddhanta gives the first point of Aries at eight degrees behind this star. Taking 72 years as the period taken by the equinoxes to recede one degree, this shows that the Surya Siddhanta speaks of a time about 576 years later, *i.e.*, 100 A.D. There is even now a difference of opinion among the Indian astronomers of about four degrees with regard to the exact position of this first point. We can only say that the Rashis were introduced into India when the Vernal equinox was somewhere between the Ashwini and the Rewati stars, a very wide period extending from 475 B.C. to about 100 A.D. It seems, however, very probable that the Rashis were introduced in India about 200 B.C., the date Dixit assigns to the oldest Indian Siddhanta (now lost of course) which uses them.

We have some further evidence to show that the Rashis were introduced about this time and not about 450 B.C. The old method of referring to time by the position of the moon among the constellations which we see in use even in the Mahabharata as it is, is also used by the Buddhistic scriptures, the Tripitakas. So far as we have gone through them there is no mention of the Rashis in any of them. The same time-honoured Nakshatras are used for calculating time, and the conclusion forces itself upon our mind that the Rashis were not in vogue in India in the days of Ashoka or at the latest in the first council of Buddhism where these Tripitakas were formulated. It seems therefore certain that the Rashis were borrowed by us about 200 B.C. from the Greeks who had invaded India long ago and whose connection was already threatening to be permanent. As the present Mahabharata mentions the Yavanas admiringly, but does not anywhere mention the Rashis, one is justified in holding that it was recast into its present shape some time between 300 and 200 B.C.

We cannot leave this subject without discussing one more reference in the Mahabharata of an astronomical character. In the Saraswati Akhyana in the Gada Parva a Vriddha or old Garga is mentioned, who, having purified his soul by austerities on the banks of the Saraswati, obtained knowledge of time and also its march of the cross motions of planets and of good and evil omens. Now an astronomer by name Garga Parashara is spoken of by Panini whose date is generally fixed at about 500 B.C. But since this Garga is called Vriddha or old, it might be supposed that a younger Garga had come into fame at the time when the Mahabharata was recast. The date of this Garga some fix at 145 B.C. from a reference in this work to the investment of Saketa by the Greeks under Menander. If this is so, then the recasting of the Mahabharata would appear to have taken place at about 140 B.C., or at the latest before 100 B.C. Garga's work, it seems, makes no mention of the Rashis, and the introduction of the Rashis must also be brought down to about after this date. If we take all the evidence heretofore detailed into consideration we may conclude generally that the Mahabharata assumed its present form between three to one hundred B.C.

CHAPTER IV.

How the Mahabharata Attained to its Present Bulk.

Having so far discussed when and why the Mahabharata was extended, we shall now proceed to discuss how it attained to its present bulk. An inquiry of this kind must necessarily be a task both difficult and delicate. Strong proof cannot be expected on a subject like this, and the suggestion that a particular chapter or story in the Mahabharata is a subsequent addition would always be distasteful and exasperating to the ear of a Hindu. But I think a criticism on the great epic cannot well be complete without an inquiry of this kind, and certain well-defined inferences naturally suggest themselves to one who studies the epic carefully—inferences which though not capable of being substantiated by irrefutable proof have still the probabilities in their favour. We shall therefore proceed to state such inferences in this chapter.

Legendary Store.—The first and the foremost reason by which the Mahabharata appears to have been extended is the ambition of Sauti, the last editor, to make it an all-embracing repository of legendary lore. In fact, he begins the Mahabharata with the assertion "Whatever is to be found here will be found elsewhere and what is not here will not be found elsewhere too." It thus seems probable that all the floating smaller legends (or Akhyanas) and historical stories (or Itihasas) which existed independently of the Bharata were brought in by Sauti so that they might not be lost or that they might be found together. It was as if a collection of old Aryan legends in a slightly modified form made for the purpose of invigorating the current cries of Aryanism, confronted as it was by Buddhism which was not slow in developing a legendary store of its own by fashioning older legends to suit its doctrines. It does not appear, however, nor is it contended that the Akhyanas and Upakhyanas, thus brought in, were all new inventions of the imagination. On the contrary it is very probable that they were older national legends which had independent existence in the form of Gathas, Itihasas and Puranas. They were nevertheless interpolations in the Mahabharata,—that is to say, they did not form part of the original Bharata of Vaishampayana or Vyasa, and their interpolated nature can well be discerned as one reads the epic. In fact, the Mahabharata itself states that the Bharata was in 24,000 verses originally and that Bharata meant the Mahabharata without the accessory legends (Upakhyanas). Nobody has found, nor has it been anywhere stated, which these Upakhyanas are, and which are the original 24,000 Shlokas. Such a statement can only be explained on the admission that there was a Bharata of 24,000 Shlokas before the Upakhyanas were added by some person later on. We shall now give some glaring examples of these subsequently added Upakhyanas.

A very typical instance of this kind of interpolation in the Saraswati Upakhyana is the Gadaparva. Herein is given an account of the Saraswati river, its rise, the tracts it flows through, the Tirthas or holy places on its banks, and their glory. It is undoubted that this is not an imaginary accouht and that it is an old legend perhaps as old as when the Saraswati was an actual river and not an imaginary bed as it now is. But all the same it is an interpolation here which does not fit in. The story of the war has reached its highest interest, the fates of the contending parties, after all the terrible loss of life, is still trembling in the balance and is about to be decided by the uncertain result of a duel between Duryodhana and Bhima, two great athletes. Balrama arrives from his pilgrimage and is hailed by both parties and asked to be a spectator. Janmejaya interrupts the story at this point and asks what were the Tirthas which Balrama visited and what was their greatness, and there is thus a digression of many chapters and many hundreds of Shlokas. One is almost exasperated at this inopportune digression, and it is certainly a very unpoetic one, of which neither Vyasa nor Vaishampayana would have been capable. The Saraswati Upakhyana has on the face of it been clumsily interpolated by Sauti, who took advantage of the mere mention of the name of the Yatra from which Balrama had returned to introduce it. Nay, there is even an independent proof of its being an interpolation. It is in this Adhyaya that many personages, whose date must be supposed to be later than that of Vyasa or Vaishampayana, such as Vriddha Garga or Shakalya and others are mentioned. Another instance of the same sort, though less glaring, is that of the Ramopakhyana in the Vana Parva. Draupadi's being carried away by Jayadratha, and being subsequently rescued and brought back, affords Sauti an occasion to introduce the story of Rama. The Upakhyana is an extensive one, perhaps the longest in the whole Mahabharata. It strikes the reader, however, as an abstract of another work which must have existed prior to it. The story is no doubt given in the words of Sauti himself whose language has a charm of its own. But that it is an interpolation is very probable from its very length. For no sensible author would give in his own work an extensive abstract of the work of another extending over 750 Shlokas.

Of Knowledge.—Sauti not only intended to make the Mahabharata a depository of learning, but also of knowledge. An instance of this is afforded by the Jambukhanda and the Bhukhanda sections in the Bheeshmaparva. The author is about to begin an account of the actual fighting in the great war, and Dhritarashtra most unpoetically asks Sanjaya the question what is the earth for which so many people are about to fight and what is its extent, and we have a geographical treatise, as it were, interpolated giving the geography of the whole world and of the Jambudwipa particularly. The description given of the universe is the usual orthodox one, perhaps prevalent in India from many centuries. But that it is an interpolation here may easily be gathered from the break in the context. At the end of Chapter 12 of the Bheeshmaparva where the Bhumikhanda ends, we have Dhritarashtra and Sanjaya talking to each other. The next chapter begins as follows:—"Thereafter Sanjaya, having returned from the battlefield after seeing everything with his own eyes, told Dhritarashtra that Bheeshma was dead." This chapter should properly have been the beginning of the Bheeshmaparva and if not the first, it should at least have been the second. For it is nowhere stated when Sanjaya went to the battlefield and when this dialogue between Sanjaya and Dhritarashtra about the extent of the world took place. Another similar instance, though not so clear, is where Narada in the beginning of the Sabhaparva asks Yudhishthira how he governs his kingdom. Here we have the whole science of political government, as it was then understood, given in the form of questions. Here we have a picture of a well-governed kingdom as it was conceived about the time of Alexander's conquest. For this science cannot have attained to such a perfection as is depicted in this chapter in days so old as the Mahabharata war.

Of Moral and Religious Teaching.—That the Mahabharata was made a vehicle of moral and religious instruction is so apparent that it hardly requires any proof. In fact, the work has almost lost its character as an epic poem and has become, and has always been acknowledged, as a Smriti and a Dharma Shastra. Native writers and authors of treatises, so old as the Brahma Sutra, quote passages from the Bharata with the feeling of reverence due to a Dharma Shastra. The leaven which has thus been introduced is so general and so extensive that it is difficult to point out to any particular section as an interpolation. The Shantiparva and the Anushasanaparva have probably been added to, to a very great extent with this object, though it is not possible to say that these Parvas are entirely new additions made about the time of the last recasting of the Bharata about 200 B.C. For certain portions of these Parvas are indeed very old as we shall have occasion to show hereafter, and it is probable that these did form part of the original Bharata. The additions made can, however, never be regretted, for here we have a vast collection of old stories, doctrines and rituals, which enables us to determine the social, moral and religious condition of the Aryas 2,000 years ago and earlier; we shall make an attempt of this kind in a subsequent book which will contain one of the most interesting inquiries undertaken in this book.

Repetition.—The second fruitful source of extension is repetition. Repetition may sometimes be useful for the purpose of impressing a subject on the reader's mind; but it must be acknowledged as a repetition. In the Mahabharata, however, we find the same story repeated twice and even thrice without any reason or acknowledgment. The repetition grates on the ear and the reader is puzzled to know why the story has been repeated and whether the author was himself aware of it. This repetition can be seen over the whole length of the work and sometimes without long intervals. Innumerable instances can be cited, but we content ourselves here with a few of them which are most striking. In the Adi Parva we have the story of Astika twice given, the second only after a few chapters after the first. The second is more detailed than the first. It seems as if Sauti was not satisfied with the meagre relation of Vaishampayana and gave the story over again with many additions, but often using the same Shlokas. The story of Kashyapa and Takshaka is also repeated, as also that of Yayati and of Pandu killing a Rishi in the guise of a deer. In the Vana Parva the Tirthas are twice enumerated, the second time with greater detail than the first. Unfortunately India was not as extensively known in the days of Vaishampayana as in the days of Sauti, and the latter probably found it necessary to make a second enumeration of the holy places in India. These and other instances of repetition made, often with very little intervals, are sometimes explained away by Janmejaya asking for greater details of the same subject or story. The 16 kings' legend is, on the other hand, an instance of repetition made at places widely separated from each other. The legend is first told, as far as we can remember, in the Drona Parva after the death of Abhimanyu, by Vyasa to Yudhishthira to console him for the sad loss he had suffered. And the same legend is told over again in the Shanti Parva by Krishna to Yudhisthira for the purpose of inducing him to lessen his grief and to enjoy the fruit of his success in war. And it is strange to see that Yudhishthira has forgotten (it is likely he may have) the story. For he asks Krishna who was Srinjaya's son and how he had died. Narada, who first told the legend to Srinjaya to console him for the death of his son and whose narration both Vyasa and Krishna had given second-hand, now comes forward and tells Yudhishthira who Srinjaya was, and how he lost and regained his son. In short, the repetition made is extremely awkward and can only take place in a vast work like the Mahabharata. The legend all the same is a very fine one, and probably very old. It is perhaps copied after the Shata-patha Brahman, Kanda 13, where a list is given of the famous kings of old who performed the Ashwamedha sacrifices. Two or three of these kings are the same, and the Shlokas in their eulogy are also almost identical.

Imitation.—The third head under which additions may be put is imitation. This is, in fact, another phase of repetition. An episode is imagined and added resembling one already existing. It is, in fact, the same feeling as has led to the composition of the many "Messengers" in imitation of the beautiful little poem of Kalidas, called the "Cloud Messenger". Very many additions can be recognised as made under this impulse. The most striking example of this is the Yaksha-prashna episode at the end of the Vana Parva. Nakul goes to drink of a pond in the jungle which is under the enchantment of a Yaksha, and drinking the water against his caution dies. Each of the remaining brothers goes in search of him, and with the exception of Yudhishthira dies similarly. Yudhishthira alone does not drink the water, and after satisfactorily answering one hundred questions put by the Yaksha succeeds in propitiating him, and the Yaksha is pleased to restore life to his brothers. The episode, one suspects, resembles the Nahusha episode already given in Chapter 195 in which Yudhishthira similary rescues his brothers from difficulty. The Yaksha-prashna episode can be proved to be an addition subsequently made, by independent considerations. For it is strange that Sahadeo, Arjuna and Bhima should each drink the water without caring to see what had happened to his predecessor, and in spite of the warning given each time by the Yaksha. It looks absurd that even the predecessor's death should not have sufficed to prove the truth of the Yaksha's warning. The questions put are, moreover, like riddles, and do not look as belonging to a great author. Further than this, there is a break in the context at this Akhyana. In this episode, which is the last in the Vana Parva, the Yaksha directs Yudhishthira to pass his days of concealment in Virata's city. And yet we find in the beginning of the next Parva that Dharma is at a loss to see where to go and live *incognito.* Again, at the end of the Yaksha-prashna episode Dharma dismisses all the Brahmans, and only the five brothers with Draupadi and Dhaumya remain ready to dive into obscurity. And yet in the beginning of the Virata Parva the Brahmans are still there and they have yet to be dismissed. These considerations would lead us to think that the story would properly run on if the Yaksha-prashna episode had not been there, in other words it has been added subsequently.

Another instance of this kind, though not quite so clear, is that of the Anu Gita. This is an episode in the Ashwamedha Parva and is fashioned after the Gita as is implied in the very name of it. Arjuna, after all the toils of the war are over, asks Shrikrishna to give him the same instructions as he had given him at the beginning of the war. Shrikrishna says that he could not rise to the same inspiration again, but would tell him what some one else had told another, and thus comes in the Anu Gita. It is naturally and admittedly not what the Gita is and preaches no new doctrine. It is probably a second-rate imitation of the Gita, and has perhaps been subsequently added.

Poetical Embellishment.—The desire for poetical embellishment has also led in a potent manner to the extension of the Mahabharata. It is natural that Sauti should have taken the advantage of every opportunity that offered itself to exhibit his poetical powers. Battles, natural sceneries and lamentations are the chief objects of a poet's delineation. The descriptions of battles in the Mahabharata are generally florid and so extended that they are often tedious. Natural sceneries have also been described with fullness, especially in the Vana Parva. The Stri Parva appears to have almost been recast. The scene, where Ghandhari having been given supernatural vision in the manner which is so usual in the Mahabharata, describes the battle-field, and the widows of fallen heroes lamenting over their dead bodies, is probably an entirely new addition. That Ghandhari should have been chosen as the person through whose mouth these lamentations are uttered, is itself quite undramatic, and Vyasa or Vaishampayana would not have committed such an error. Moreover, the description and lamentations are somewhat sensual in taste, much in the fashion of later Sanskrit poets, the well-known Shloka "Ayam sa rasanotkarshi," &c., being found here. Further, it is improbable that these bereaved women would have been allowed to roam over the battle-field, covered as it must have been by indistinguishable masses of bones of men and animals, and it is also improbable that dead bodies could have been capable of identification as they were allowed to lie on the battle-field for many days, exposed to hungry beasts and birds of prey. How, for instance, can Abhimanyu's face be still fresh and shining as it is being kissed by his young wife? The whole scene is improbable, undramatic and unbecoming. A similar attempt may be discerned in the Virata Parva where scenes and female beauties are described with much more elaboration than elsewhere. But the scenes are here also undramatic as they do not bear out and develop the characters as they are conceived. For example, Uttara who a little while ago was a timid boy, as soon as Arjuna discloses himself, becomes a brave man and a poet too. His description of the bows of the five brothers as they are taken down from the tree where they are concealed, is very beautiful indeed, and two of the Shlokas are very fine riddles also.

Here we may conveniently treat of the Kuta or riddle Shlokas. They appear to have been introduced by Sauti under the same impulse, *viz.*, the desire to exhibit poetical powers. It is affirmed in the beginning of the Mahabharata that there are 8,800 Kuta Shlokas in all throughout the whole work, which gives one Shloka for every 12. It appears therefore probable that this number has been exaggerated. In the appendix are given as many Kuta Shlokas as we could find out while reading the work. Some of these Shlokas are really very ingenious and the two Shlokas in which Uttara describes two bows may be taken as the best examples of them. The riddle lies generally in the use of a word which has two meanings; the most obvious of them occurring to the rèader first and thus throwing him off the scent. The worst example of such Kuta Shlokas, perhaps an interpolation of even a later date than Sauti, is to be found in the Karna Parva, Chapter 90. The Shloka No. 40 is a long metred (Shardul-vikridita) Shloka and uses the word "Gau" with its many meanings many times.

Anticipation.—Anticipation or suggestion of events is a poetical art which authors are fond of using, and the Mahabharata is not without examples of it. The last editor Sauti has made several additions with this object. We have an instance of this in the Stri Parva where Gandhari is made to curse Shrikrishna for not having prevented the terrible slaughter shown by the state of the battle-field, that he too and his race would fight among themselves and slaughter one another. This scene in the Stri Parva, as we have already seen, is wholly an interpolation. Similarly before the beginning of the fight Dharma Raja goes to each one of the commanders on the opposite side and asks him how he could kill him, whereon each one anticipates the manner in which he was subsequently killed. Now this is very probably an interpolation; it is derogatory to the character of not only Yudhishthira but also to that of these great commanders; for it represents them as traitors. Moreover it is ludicrous to represent Yudhishthira asking openly so imbecile a question. To Shalya Yudhishthira is made to say that he should make the Tejobhanga of Karna (dis-spirit him) when he would be asked to act as a charioteer to him. This is carrying the *Bija sowing* or poetical anticipation to an absurd length. Could anybody have then predicted that Shalya would be asked by Karna to drive his chariot on the battle-field, and even if it were so probable, would anybody have thought that mere discouragement of Karna would have assisted the cause of Yudhishthira? Even as the Mahabharata is, Shalya is not represented as acting so meanly. On the contrary he does his self-imposed duty most faithfully and protects and assists Karna whenever necessary.

Explanation.—The last category under which additions appear to have been made is explanation of extraordinary conduct. Lapse of thousands of years between the events and the last recasting of the Mahabharata made it necessary that certain actions should be explained away and Sauti appears to have added chapters here and there for this purpose. The most palpable addition under this head is the chapter wherein Vyasa seeks to explain to Drupada how it is that the five Pandavas may marry a single woman. The Pandavas are alleged to be all Indras (which is itself inconsistent with the idea stated elsewhere in the Mahabharata that Arjuna alone was Indra) and when Drupada is not satisfied even then, the usual device, *viz.*, the gift of supernatural vision is adopted and Drupada sees that they are all Indras. Bhima's drinking warm blood from the throat of Dusshasana is also sought to be explained away in the Stri Parva, Chapter 15, where it is suggested that he only made a feint of drinking the blood but did not actually do it in fulfilment of his vow.

Vyasa's Appearance now and then.—Vyasa's frequent appearance on the scene, of course by his supernatural powers, appears to have been arranged for the purpose of such explanation. He also often comes to warn, to advise and to console actors without apparent necessity or result. For instance, at the time of Duryodhana's birth Vyasa appears on the scene and warns Dhritarashtra of the evils of which he would be the cause and advises him without success to throw him into the Ganges. So again when the war is about to begin Vyasa appears before Dhritarashtra and tells him what evil omens are happening and how the war would be a dreadful one. Here are introduced a fresh (many having been already mentioned in the Udyoga Parva) number of evil omens and inauspicious conjunctions of planets which are probably imaginary and which have created a confusion of which we shall have to speak later on. The appearance of Vyasa is generally of no avail and the march of events is in no way hindered without it.

Such are the principal heads under which additions appear to have been made by Sauti in recasting the Mahabharata. It is by no means suggested that the list is exhaustive or that the examples cited are the only examples of them. Two examples only have been given under each head so that the subject may not be tedious to the reader who is not supposed to have read the Mahabharata. It would be tiresome to the general reader, to give here an exhaustive list of such chapters and episodes as appear to have been added at the time of the last recasting of the Bharata, and we give in the Appendix a note in which this subject has been discussed in detail.

Notwithstanding the additions thus made it must be said to the credit of Sauti that he has succeeded in moulding a work of such an enormous extent into a harmonious and consistent whole. It is only rarely that we come across discrepancies, contradictions or breaks in the context. In fact they are rarer in the Mahabharata than in the Ramayana. In two places, however, Sauti has betrayed himself hopelessly. In the Bhishma Parva, where Yudhishthira asks Shalya to discourage Karna, an episode which we have already shown to be an addition, he is made to say "Carry out your promise made in Udyoga," by which is presumably meant the Udyogaparva. Now it is absurd to represent an actor giving a reference to a division of the drama or epic itself. Similarly Kunti in the Ashwamedha Parva, Chapter 66, requests Shrikrishna to carry out his promise made in "Aishika" (a previous Parva), *viz.*, to resuscitate the child of Uttara if born dead. How Sauti could have put these references to the Parvas of the epic in the mouth of the actors it is difficult to explain, except on the supposition that the enormous length of the epic made it pardonable even for the actors to give references to its divisions.

CHAPTER V.

The Vaishnavite Element in the Mahabharata.

Allied with the subject of the preceding chapter is the question whether the Mahabharata was originally Vaishnavite, how the Vaishnavite element grew in it and what is its present attitude towards the Vaishnavite creed. It is an extremely interesting inquiry and, however distasteful or delicate it may be from the religious point of view, we cannot shirk it.

That Vyasa was an admirer of Shrikrishna and a worshipper of Vishnu appears clear from the very first verse of invocation which we cannot attribute to any one but Vyasa. Therein the God Narayana is invoked and is also identified with Shrikrishna. It may perhaps be necessary to state here that at the time of Vyasa, which is the same as the time of the Brahmanas, the Vedic Rishis had come to give predominance to Vishnu and to ignore the precedence of Indra so conspicuous in the Mantra portion of the Vedas, and we may believe it readily that Vyasa but reflected the general sentiment of the Rishis of the Brahmana period. There was another school which was trying to give predominance among gods to Shiva as we can see from the Atharva Mandukya Upanishad, where instead of the words Tad Vishnoh Parâmam Pandam wê have the Supreme Being as typified in "One" called Shiva. This school appears to have been, however, in the minority, and the Rishis of the Brahmanic period laid down the diction (*see* the beginning of the Aitareya Brahmana of the Rig Veda) that among gods Agni or Fire was the last and Vishnu was the first. Shrikrishna, about whose personality and preachings we shall speak in a separate book, was a contemporary of Vyasa and was believed to be an Avatara or incarnation of Vishnu. Vyasa was probably one of those who believed so, and it is not at all impossible that the Itihasa or history called "Triumph" which he wrote was pervaded with the feeling of admiration which he entertained for him. We are therefore not stretching our guess too far when we hold that the original poem of Vyasa was written in glorification of Krishna or Narayana as of Arjuna or Nara.

It must, however, be granted that Krishna worship was, as may naturally be expected, in its infancy when Vyasa wrote his poem ; and we find one or two places in the Mahabharata where Krishna is treated as an ordinary mortal. The statements which we are now going to refer strike us as invaluable fossils which are preserved in this vast work by mistake or accident and which give evidence of the fact that the original work of Vyasa was considerably different from its present form. In the Mausala Parva, where, after the Yadavas had been destroyed in a terrible internecine feud, Arjuna is said to have led away the many wives of Krishna, it is stated that barbarians attacked Arjuna and carried away many from among his fair charge. "Some," it is added, "went away of their own choice." Now had the author been thoroughly Vaishnavite he would not have represented some of Krishna's wives or rather women as eloping with the barbarians, although it is but natural to expect, where a man keeps an unwieldy harem, some of the women to be dissatisfied and in a mood to elope. But this fact is detrimental to the greatness of Shrikrishna as an incarnation of Vishnu. Probably Vyasa here pointed out the only foible in his character great as it was and was not hindered by any particular sentiments from expressing his opinions freely. Similarly in the Gada-Parva where Duryodhana was, as he lay wounded on the battle-field, upbraided by Shrikrishna for his evil deeds, the former exculpated himself in a vigorous speech and exclaimed that he had lived a brilliant life and died a brilliant death, levelled down when fighting honourably by a dishonourable blow dealt by one of those who wished to pose as honourable men. The poet adds: "The gods showered flowers on the dying man in approbation and all those present felt abashed." It is strange that we should find in the Mahabharata a work which glorifies Shrikrishna in every possible manner, a remark of this kind, strange that the gods of Heaven expressed their approval of the conduct of Duryodhana, conduct so vehemently denounced by Shrikrishna himself. It seems clear that Vyasa did not always side with Krishna but expressed his sentiments without bias.

Vaishampayana was probably a more pronounced follower of the Vaishnavite creed than Vyasa. For his Bharata is recognised by the Vaishnavas to have along with the Pancharatras, a special work belonging to that sect, the same sanctity as the Vedas themselves. The inclusion of the Bhagwat Gita and the Vishnu Sahasra Nama in the Bharata is probably the chief reason why it is held in so much reverence by the Vaishnavas. The Bhagwat Gita, undoubtedly the most precious book in non-Vedic Sanskrit literature, contains, in our opinion, the preaching of Shrikrishna, though not in his own words, but in the words of Vyasa. It may have been re-arranged and altered here and there by Vaishampayana and made more Vaishnavite in appearance. But it is pre-eminently the thought of Shrikrishna clothed in the language of Vyasa. The Vishnu Sahasra Nama may be attributed to Vaishampayana being more antique than the rest of the poem as we can judge from the language.

What other additions and alterations Vaishampayana made in order to strengthen the cause of Krishna worship it is not easy to detect at this distance of time ; but the critical reader of the Mahabharata cannot but be convinced that the Vaishnavite element is constantly accumulating. Krishna is glorified and praised whenever opportunity offers, and the usual story of Avataras given in the Puranas, namely, that the earth, oppressed, goes to Vishnu in the form of a cow to implore for redress, and he comes to life together with all the deities of heaven for the purpose of destroying her oppressors, is found, though not in so many words, in the Bharata in a nucleus form. In Chapters 65 and 66 of the Bhishma Parva we have the theory of incarnation as believed in by the Vaishnavas given by the mouth of Bhishma, who wishes to impress on Duryodhana's mind, perhaps unsuccessfully, the greatness of Shrikrishna. "Brahma, surrounded by Rishis and gods, suddenly saw burning light before him and praised Vishnu, the Supreme

Being, and implored him to be born for the deliverance of the earth. Vishnu thereon was pleased and promised to grant his request." Here are mentioned the four names of Vishnu which are invested with special meanings among the Vaishnavas, *viz.*, Vasudeva, Sankarshana, Pradyumna and Anirudhha, from the last of whom is said to have been born Brahma, the creator himself. The Devarishis and the Gandharvas were astonished and did not know, it is said, with whom Brahma held converse, and Brahma explained to them what had happened.

But a different and somewhat quaint account of Vishnu's incarnation is to be found in Chapter 197 of the Adi Parva. It is probably the earlier version and preserved in the Mahabharata by accident or by a feeling of reverence for old texts in the same manner as other old texts already referred to have been saved. The story is well worth giving in full. Vyasa explains to king Drupada how the five Pandavas can marry one single woman. The gods once performed a sacrifice at which the god of death officiated as the Sharnitra (killer). Mortals consequently did not die and multiplied immensely. Indra and others being afraid went to Prajapati and said "We are afraid of men for, there is now no difference between mortals and immortals." Prajapati replied "When the god of death will finish his work he will destroy men." Indra went to see the sacrifice and on the way saw a golden lotus coming down the Ganges. Wishing to know whence it came, he went to the source and saw a beautiful woman weeping and standing in the stream to take water. Her tear fell in the stream and became a golden lotus immediately. Indra asked her why she wept and she requested him to follow her. He saw Shiva with his wife playing at dice and being disregarded exclaimed "I am the Lord of the Universe." Shiva looked at him and only laughed. Indra raised his hand but it was made motionless. Shiva then said "You are proud. Look into that cave. There are four previous Indras' confined there. Go you all to the earth and be born as mortals. This damsel who is the prosperity of heaven will be your wife." Indra trembled and consented. They then went to Narayana, the Lord of the Universe, and told him what had happened. He too snatched two hairs, one white and the other black, from his body and they were laid in the womb of Devaki and Rhohini, the two queens of Vasudeva. Thus were born Balrama, the white, from the white hair and Krishna from the black one. The five Indras became the five Pandavas and the Laxmi of heaven is Draupadi. The commentator explains that the word hair meant semin and that Krishna was born directly of Hari or Narayana. He tries in this way to explain the apparent discrepancy from the modern belief, *viz.*, that Krishna was a full and not a partial Avatara. But other discrepancies still remain. Balrama is not now believed to be an Avatara of Vishnu, though in the above he is shown to be as full an Avatara as Krishna himself. Moreover there is not that subordination of Prajapati and of Shiva to Vishnu in the above account which is to be found in the usual version. The Pandavas too are all looked upon as Indras and Draupadi is merely the prosperity of heaven.

All these defects have been corrected in the account given in the Amshavatara, Chapter 167 of the Adi Parva, where every actor in the Mahabharata is shown to be the partial incarnation of some god or demon. It is the third version most probably adjusted by Sauti. Therein the oppressed earth goes to Brahma who directs all gods to go down to the earth and be born as mortals. They then all go to Narayana, and Indra implores him to be born on the earth by Amsha, and they make a compact and the gods are born by Amsha or portion only in the families of Kings and Brahmanas. In the list given hereafter Balrama is said to be born of Shesha and Draupadi is said to be born of Shachi, the wife of Indra. The sixteen thousand wives of Krishna are here said to be born of the Apsaras by the order of Indra. In Chapter 5 of the Swargarohana Parva the actors are said to have returned after death to the respective deities from whom they sprang. These women are said after death to have been united with the Apsaras, a thing which we can scarcely reconcile with the statement about some of them referred to above.

The Vaishnava sect or creed, which is based on Krishna worship, began with Krishna and gathered strength as time rolled on. In the days of Magesthenes it was a fully established creed, and it is recorded by that historian that the god Heracles was worshipped by the Shoursene people who had two important cities, *viz.*, Methora and Chimbothro. It is difficult to identify the last, but the Shoursene people were those who were descended from Shurasena, the father of Krishna, and they lived in or about Mathura, which is even now the centre of Krishna worship. It is but natural to expect that the Bharata of Vaishampayana, which is pre-eminently concerned with the doings of Krishna as well as with the exploits of Arjuna, gathered accumulations as time went on in support of that creed. It will suffice if we quote two more examples, *viz.*, the Bhishmastavaraja, which is perhaps one of the best praises of the supreme deity, and the Narayanastramoksha Parva.

But the worship of Shiva was as firmly established in the days of Magesthenes as the worship of Vishnu, and Sauti, who was concerned with the defence of the whole of the orthodox religion, as it then existed, against Buddhism, had to introduce episodes and anecdotes in glorification of Shiva also. If the Bharata of Vaishampayana was distinctly Vaishnavite it appears to us that the Mahabharata of Sauti is distinctly non-sectarian. It is this aspect of the work as it exists to-day that has made it dear to all Hindus, and all creeds alike claim it as their sacred book. It is this unifying spirit which is the charm of this vast work from a philosophic point of view. In the Anushásana Parva is to be found the Akhyana of Upamanyu in praise of Shiva, and the beauty of it is that the story is related by Krishna himself. In Chapters 14—18 we find that Krishna went and performed austerities in the Himalayas and pleased Shankar and obtained a son for his wife Jambuvati. The 1,000 names of Shiva are here given, as recited originally by Tundi and told to Krishna by Upamanyu. Rishis are also mentioned as praising Shiva and obtaining boons. The unification of Shiva, Vishnu, and Brahma, as it is believed in by orthodox Hinduism, is also clearly apparent in this Akhyana, for it is stated that the Supreme Being sent forth Brahma from his right side to create the world and Vishnu from his left to protect it and Rudra at the time of its end. That Sauti introduced this Akhyana is, however, certain from its evident isolation in context, the language of these chapters and the frequent change in the metre. Krishna again is said by Bhishma to have performed austerities for a thousand years. This is extremely improbable, for no actor in the Mahabharata is represented as of fabulous age. Their ages are the ordinary ages of human beings as they are now. Krishna even according to popular belief was only 84 years and according to another theory 123 years old when the Mahabharata fight took place. All these circumstances lead us to think that this Upamanyu Akhyana is an addition made by Sauti.

In many other places, chapters and incidents are introduced in praise of Shiva. In the Dronaparva, when Arjuna had vowed to kill Jayadratha and Drona had vowed to save him, Krishna thought that it was necessary to fortify Arjuna by a boon from Shiva, and Arjuna is said to have gone in Samadhi to Shiva and obtained from him the Pashupatastra, Chapters 90 and 91. (This is rather strange as Arjuna had already got the Astra in Vanaparva where his fight with Shiva is so beautifully described.) In this incident also the beauty is that it is with the advice of Krishna that Arjuna contemplates Shiva, and in the contemplation both go to Shiva and praise him. Similarly when Ashwatthama is about to begin his night massacre of the sleeping survivors of the war he propitiates Shiva by offering himself as an oblation and obtains from him a deadly sword (Chapter 7, Saupticparva). Here too Shankar says that Krishna is dear to him for many reasons and his devotion to Shankar among them. At the end of this Parva we have a reference to, and explanation of, the Linga worship, and there again the greatness of Shiva is described by the mouth of Krishna himself. It seems clear that all these references to Shiva worship are made in a spirit of unifying the diverse sects that existed when Sauti finally recast this poem. We find the Vaishnava and Pashupata sects, with their peculiar tenets in particular point, discussed and refuted in the Brahma Sutras also, which cannot be supposed to be later than the beginning of the Christian Era. It is probably in the same spirit that Sauti made these additions and others in praise of Devi (Bhishmaparva) and Surya (Vanaparva) and Kartikeya (Vanaparva), who are all looked upon as different manifestations of the Supreme Being. The Mahabharata as it is, consequently, cannot be looked upon as Vaishnavite, though it was perhaps so in the beginning and though the Vaishnavite element had been accumulating[1] before its final redaction. The Vaishanvas who look upon Bharata as one of their Scriptures are now driven to explain these praises of other gods as introduced to delude the world!

[1] Bhagvat-Gita, the 1,000 Names of Vishnu, the Prayer of Bhishma, the Rescue of the Elephant, and Anusmriti are said to be the five jewels to be found in the Bharata. The Rescue of the Elephant is to be found in a clearly interpolated manner in one of the Bombay editions, while the last is to be found nowhere.

CHAPTER VI.

MAHABHARATA AS AN EPIC POEM.

DIVESTED of these additions and accumulations the Mahabharata indeed deserves to rank among the finest epic poems of the world. The epic poem which has ever been regarded as in its nature the most noble of all poetic performances must conform, in the words of Arnold, to the following conditions :—"The subject of the epic poem must be some *one*, great, complex action. The principal personages must belong to the high places of society and must be grand and elevated in their ideas. The measure must be of a sonorous dignity befitting the subject. The epic is developed by a mixture of dialogue, soliloquy and narration." We shall try to see how far these requisites which have been laid down since the days of Aristotle are fulfilled by the Mahabharata.

The subject of this poem is the great war fought on the plain of Kurukshetra by the Pandavas and the Kauravas, two sections of the same race, assisted by the various nations of the whole of India as it was then known. This subject is introduced by the poet in the very first verse of invocation. "Having saluted the god Narayana and Nara, the best of men, and the goddess of speech, let us recite the 'Triumph.'" Here Vyasa at once introduces us to the chief actors of his poem and his subject, *viz.*, the victory gained by them, just like Homer, who begins his Illiad with the name of Achilles, the hero of his poem, and his wrath the subject of it. Sauti does not fail in developing this art of the original author in his introduction and takes us at once to the subject of the poem. "I have visited," says he to Shaunak, "the far-famed battle-field, my curiosity having been excited by the stories I had heard about the great war from the mouth of Vaishampayana at the great Sarpa-satra (Serpent-sacrifice) of Janmejaya." The subject of our poem then is the great Bharata war.

It may perhaps be objected that the subject of the Mahabharata is not one great action but is rather in the nature of the life of a hero. The Mahabharata no doubt gives the life of the Pandavas from beginning to end and should thus be classed a heroic rather than an epic poem. It seems, however, clear that the poet's principal object is not to give a life of the Pandavas. The primary theme which the poet has set before himself is the great war. The events which lead up to the great war are a necessary part of the subject and have therefore been described in detail. The events which happened after the war, such as the performance of the horse-sacrifice and the Pandavas' final departure on their great journey, have undoubtedly no connection with the real theme. But the poet has given them merely for the purpose of satisfying the curiosity of the reader, for it is remarkable that these scenes have been described with a brevity and meagreness of detail which is in evident contrast with the rest of the poem. It is therefore, not improper if we take it that the subject of the Mahabharata, which has been classed by all writers as an epic poem, is the great war and not the life of the Pandavas.

That this subject is complex, nobody will ever be disposed to deny. In fact, the word Mahabharata raises up in our mind the idea of a something which is vast and extremely diversified. But very few have realised the vastness and the complexity of the subject from a poetic point of view. The scenes and incidents in the Mahabharata suitable for poetic treatment are so numerous and diverse, that scarcely any interesting scene has ever been conceived by modern Sanskrit poets which has not its parent in the Mahabharata. "Like the big Banian tree," Sauti himself boasts in the beginning of the poem, "the Mahabharata is the resting place for all modern poets." It is the perennial stream from which any poet may drink and derive inspiration.

The incidents in the Mahabharata, very numerous and deversified as they are, have been so well knit together in one story that it is not possible to conceive of a. plot more splendid and well laid. It has often occurred to me that if the story of the Mahabharata is not a historical one it must indeed be the production of an imagination which is higher than that of Shakespeare. Diversity of characters and their truthfulness to nature which characterise Shakespeare's plays are to be found in the Mahabharata also; but the wonder is that so many characters have been brought together in one plot. What Shakespeare exhibits in many dramas

Vyasa has brought together in one vast plot, the parts of which in spite of their vastness are like the limbs of an elephant set together in one harmonious and graceful whole.

It is well known that particular instances in the Mahabharata have furnished subjects to later Sanskrit poets for their epics and dramas which are poetically complete in themselves. It is well known that modern Kathekaries or Rhapsodists base their declamations lasting for hours together on single incidents in this vast fabric. But it is not well known that the story of the epic is not only vast and well knitted but is capable of still further development. In fact, the poet has constantly kept the chief subject, *viz.*, the great war, before him and has not allowed himself to be drawn away by the allurements for extension which the plot afforded. Only one illustration would suffice to show what I mean. Duryodhana's wife appears nowhere on the scene in the Mahabharata. Nay her name even, which later poets have given as Bhanumati, so far as I can remember, is not found there. There is no scene in the Mahabharata like that in the Illiad between Hector and Andromache, a scene often copied by later poets, in which a brave warrior, who is about to engage in battle and is not very sanguine about the result, is taking leave of his noble and loving wife. It may be observed that the author of the Mahabharata exhibits better art in avoiding such a scene, for the implacable and proud character of the hero's adversary is thus better sustained. We shall return to this subject again.

The greatness of the subject of the Mahabharata, like its complexity, is also beyond dispute. The great war, as it is usually called, ended in the total destruction of two vast armies, such was the dogged determination and the uncompromising hatred of the opposite parties. The war was further a memorable event. It marked the beginning of a decrepit age, at least so far as India is concerned, as history has but too truly proved. Although then, the subject cannot compare with the subject of the Paradise Lost, the interest of which transcends the limits of a nation, it may well compare with the theme of Homer's Illiad. The Mahabharata was, and still is, the national poem of India as the Illiad was of Greece. It is the store-house of Indian genealogy, mythology and antiquity.

Having thus far spoken about the subject of our epic poem we shall now speak of the characters. One cannot sufficiently admire the personages whose noble actions and high ideas the Mahabharata most effectively describes. Yudhisthira, Bhima, Arjuna, Karna, Draupadi, Drona and, above all, Bhishma, to leave out of question Shrikrishna, have been and shall be for all time to come models of greatness and virtue, ever inspiring the Aryan mind in India to deeds of self-sacrifice in the performance of duty. Even Duryodhana has a charm and splendour of his own. His unswerving determination, his ambition which knows no medium between death and the Imperial crown, are brought out most vividly by the poet and teach a lesson of their own. And here we may notice the superiority of the poet's delineation of character over Homer or even

Milton. The adversary of the hero in the Illiad or in the Paradise Lost has been so depicted that instead of creating disgust he enlists our sympathy. "Against his will," observes Arnold about Milton, "for he seems well aware and is continually reminding himself that Satan ought to be represented as purely evil, yet he continually places language in his mouth—language which is inconsistent with such a conception." Similarly with Homer's Hector the reader is not only pleased but is very often sympathising. The reader half feels for the brave warrior, who is trying in vain to save his country and his kingdom, though involved in a wrong cause. As already observed, the beautiful picture which Homer has portrayed of the noble wife of Hector and the fervid love with which he snatches a kiss of his innocent child, though in itself a grand poetic scene, has marred the general purpose of the poem. The readers of Paradise Lost or of the Illiad are half tempted to think that Satan or Hector is the hero of the poem and not Adam or Achilles.

The female characters of the Mahabharata again strike us as superior to those of the Illiad. Helen and even Andromache cannot rival Draupadi. We cannot sufficiently admire the stately character which the author of the Mahabharata has built up in the person of Draupadi. She is a noble woman, ever conscious of her dignity, never losing her temper in the worst of her trials, chaste and pure beyond all thought. But she is human still. She often discusses the situation with all the vehemence of a female's susceptible temper. She often insists upon things which her husbands are sometimes compelled to accept. She is not, however, lowly and fit to be discussed to the distaff as Hector does his wife. She is a Rajput woman with the Rajput's bravery and determination illuminating her face. Nay when Kichaka or Jayadratha try to seize and take undue liberty with her, with the impulse of a Rajput woman she gives them a push which throws them down. She has a presence of mind which even men may be proud of. For instance, she loses not a moment in telling Karna when he rises to string the bow at the Swayamvara, that she does not wish to marry a charioteer. And when she is alleged to have been won at the disgraceful game at dice she asks a question which confounds the courtiers of Duryodhana. Above all, her noble willingness to share the fortunes of Arjuna disguised as a poor Brahmin when he won her at the Swayamvara, or when she followed the Pandavas in the forest in their long exile, has always inspired Hindu women with courage and contentment in sharing the lot of their husbands.

Kunti is another strong female character in the Mahabharata. Although she remains in Vidura's house when the Pandavas with their wife go into 12 years' exile, the message which she sends with Krishna to her sons is in true Rajput fashion and is one of the most stirring calls to fight. She wishes her sons either to die or conquer. She, however, does not incite her sons to fight for her sake. When the Pandavas are successful and established on the throne she leaves them and accompanies Dhritarashtra to the forest and dies in the performance of her duties, *viz.*, attendance on the blind old man. As she starts Bhima implores her to stay and enjoy the fruit of her advice, but she firmly replies : "I have had enjoyment enough during my husband's time. I incited you to fight because I did not wish you to beg." Her last parting advice to her sons may be written in golden letters : "Believe in righteousness. Have minds ever great." It is the purport of the whole Mahabharata condensed into one single line.

The female characters of the Mahabharata, elevated as they are, have a touch of humanity which makes the whole world kin. When Arjuna brings his second wife Subhadra to Indraprastha, Draupadi expresses her feeling of jealousy in a happy metaphor : "The first tie however firm and strong relaxes when followed by another." Kunti when Karna appears in the lists of the tournament faints. Uttara asking Arjuna to accompany her brother on his expedition against the Kauravas requests him to bring good pieces of cloth for the use of her dolls, never doubting that her brother would conquer their mighty hosts. These and other touches of the poet, illustrative of feminine weakness, make the female characters of the Mahabharata all the more lovable.

Thirdly, the divine characters in the Mahabharata are, unlike those in the Illiad, really divine and not comic. It has generally been remarked that if there are any comic scenes in the Illiad, for there is little room for comic scenes in the grave march of an epic poem, they are those on the top of the Olympus. The gods in heaven squabble over affairs on the earth; they assist mortals in the most whimsical manner for very low motives. Even Jove, the Almighty God, is often distracted by the importunities of his wife Juno, who has peculiar partialities of her own, and has sometimes to threaten her with corporal chastisement. The gods in the Mahabharata are much like the gods of the Greeks, but the poet never dethrones them from their high position. He introduces them with great effect into the poem and adds to the diversity of its characters. The gods of Vyasa rarely interfere with human affairs. If ever they do, they act as gods and not as selfish human beings. We may cite one instance. Indra is represented as going to Karna to deprive him of his natural armour, said to have been born with him, in order that his son, Arjuna, might not find him invulnerable in battle. Karna is well known as a donor who refuses nothing to Brahmanas, and Indra in the disguise of a Brahmana asks Karna to part with his armour. The generous man gives it to him knowing who he is. The Mahabharata does not represent Indra as walking off quietly with it, but as acting like a god. He is pleased and like a god grants a boon. Karna asks for a weapon from him which is infallible against one mortal, and Indra grants one to him not caring that it might be used against Arjuna himself. Again Arjuna's visit to the heavens or Indra's court and his encounter with and propitiation of Shiva—an incident which Bharavi has developed into his Mahakavya, the Kirata-Arjuniya—are described by the Mahabharata in a few brilliant touches and the divine characters act like gods and not men.

We will now pass to the question how Vyasa develops his characters and his story. We may repeat the part of the definition of an epic poem given by Arnold. The epic is developed by a mixture of dialogue, soliloquy and narrative. The author of the Mahabharata is equally strong in this as in the other characteristics of the epic poem. The Mahabharata is peculiarly powerful in its dialogues. In fact, we look upon the dialogue as the strong point of the poem. As in the Illiad or the Paradise Lost the speeches here are well conceived, eloquent and forcible and are suited to the character of the speakers. It is not possible to give here any particular dialogues *in extenso*, and we can only refer to some of the most brilliant speeches: such as the dialogue in the Adiparva between Duryodhana, Karna, Arjuna and Bhima on the occasion of the exhibition of their skill in archery; or the dialogue in the Sabha Parva between Shisupal and Bhishma, at the end of which Krishna killed Shisupala by the throw of his discus; or the dialogue in the Vana Parva between Yudhishthira, Bhima and Draupadi, the latter advising the use of stratagem to oppose stratagem; or the dialogue in the Drona Parva between Dhrishtdyumna, Satyaki, Arjuna and Yudhishthira when the former had killed Drona in a defenceless condition. Krishna's address to the Kauravas on the occasion of his mediation for peace is a master-piece and may alone suffice to give the casual reader an idea of Vyasa's power of conceiving a powerful speech. Another example of Krishna's masterly speeches is the one in the Karna Parva wherein he tries to rouse the spirits of Arjuna as he advances to battle with Karna. These and other speeches, too numerous to mention, are a peculiar charm of the poem and almost convert it into a drama.

One peculiar trait of the speeches in the Mahabharata is their fearlessness. They are utterances of outspoken truthful persons who are not afraid to tell their hearers what they think of them. Vidura, for instance, is never afraid to upbraid Duryodhana in the strongest terms possible whenever he is doing a wrong act. But perhaps Vidura's position and relation were a shield to him. Shakuntala had no such shield. The Shakuntala of Vyasa is a far different being from the Shakuntala of Kalidas. She is a country girl outspoken and fearless and conscious of the dignity of virtue. When the king denied in open court having ever seen, much less married her, she said: "I disclaim to keep company with you who have no respect for truth. Truth is more precious than husband or son." She does not swoon like the gentle heroine of Kalidasa's famous drama but leaves the court in disgust.

The conversation between Shalya and Karna in the Karna Parva is another instance of the out-spoken character of the speeches which Vyasa puts in the mouths of his characters. The story of a swan and crow is a splendid animal story told for the purpose of illustrating a moral and is well worth a perusal. In fact Vyasa contrives to teach the highest morals through the mouth of his characters, his poem furnishing illimitable sayings and examples on the value of truthfulness, simplicity, honour, devotion to duty, generosity and self-restraint. There is one feeling or virtue, which is, however, not touched, *viz.*, patriotism, which forms a peculiar charm of some of the speeches in the Illiad. Probably the Aryans of India did not develop political virtues like their brethren of the West, or perhaps the theme of the Mahabharata did not afford opportunities for patriotic utterances, being a war between two sections of the same race.

We now come to soliloquy. The Sanskrit poets have not much used this form of speech except in the drama where also the 'Swagatas' are short and not very eloquent. The Mahabharata does not contain any soliloquy unless we can call the lamentations of Duryodhana as he lay wounded on the battle-field a soliloquy. We think soliloquy is not a natural form of utterance. One may sometimes think loudly, but very few, perhaps none give utterance to a sustained and impassioned speech when thinking to themselves. We are not, however, going to launch upon a controversy. It is enough to note that there are no soliloquies in the Mahabharata.

In narrative the author of the Mahabharata displays as great a power as Homer or Milton. The story is always told with force and perspicuity and the descriptions are often picturesque and grand. In relating the details of fighting especially Vyasa discovers a power which is almost unique. The descriptions of the individual duels in the Mahabharata, one may be disposed to observe, are full of repetition; one warrior throwing so many arrows at another who returns the so many, being the usual way of describing a duel and when the same scenes are repeated the reader is apt to get tired. Something of the same kind happens even in the Illiad. But we must transport ourselves to those ancient days when the chief offensive weapon was the arrow or the javelin, and when battles usually took the form of duels between opposite chiefs. Even as it is, the variety of the scenes which the poet conceives and the vigour with which they are described are really wonderful. The recitation of the Mahabharata, especially the war portion of it, like that of the Illiad, always roused the martial spirits of the hearers, and it is well-known that Shivaji drew his heroic inspiration from a hearing of this poem.

In the description of natural scenes, the Mahabharata is not as successful as the Ramayana. There are very few descriptions of this kind in the whole poem. In the Vanaparva, however, we have a description of the Himalayas which strikes us as coming from the pen of one who has seen or lived on the snow-clad northern barrier of India. The description of an avalanche in which the Pandavas and Draupadi were caught is so graphic and real, that we feel as if we are reading the newspaper report of snow-storms which even in these days occasionally overtake a Mail Tonga, sometimes with fatal results. In the description of the Gandha Madana hill, however, though very picturesque and full, we discover some touches added by Sauti as we find the Tal or the Palm trees mentioned among the trees adorning the hill, which seems to be drawn more from imagination than reality.

In describing persons the Mahabharata is chaste and powerful. Female beauty is nowhere described in a sensual manner as is so habitual with later Sanskrit poets. The description of Draupadi which Yudhishthira gives when he stakes her at the game of dice is in the best fashion of Vyasa. "Draupadi," says he, "neither tall nor short, neither lean nor stout, with eyes as large and with breath as fragrant as an autumnal lotus, in temper, in beauty even as a man could ever wish his wife to be, she who goes to bed after and rises before me, her I stake Shakuni, come, play." Even the praise of Draupadi's charms which the poet puts in the mouth of Kichaka are not as turbid as one could have expected them from his mouth. Arjuna, disguised as Brihannada or a eunuch, is most charmingly and correctly described; so also Bhishma and Drona as they go to battle and Karna as he enters the lists in the Adiparva. These instances would suffice as illustrations.

The last point for consideration is the measure and the language of the poem. The Mahabharata is mostly told in the Anushtub metre and the Upajati metre is also frequently used. These are the recognised metres of an epic poem in the Sanskrit language. The well-known Mahakavyas are composed in these metres with a sprinkling of other metres. The Anushtub metre has lost in dignity owing to the use of it in the Puranas, the Upa-puranas, in works on sciences and on art. It is apparently an hackneyed and easy metre. But we must remember that in the hands of capable authors Anushtub Shlokas are still dignified and powerful and we need only instance Kalidasa's Raghuvamsha, Cantos 1 and 4. Like the Iambic in English the Anushtub, though the recognised metre for all heroic or epic works, gains or loses in dignity according as the author is a real poet or a mere versifier.

The language of the Mahabharata is also dignified and fit for an epic poem. It is distinguished by three characteristics: simplicity, depth and correctness. Simplicity and depth are indeed two things which can rarely be combined. Later Mahakavyas are distinguished by dignity of expression but they have attained to it at the expense of perspicuity. The reader is charmed and pleased by the sound, but he has to stop and ponder over the letters before he gets at the meaning. It is not so in the Mahabharata. Later Puranas may compare well with the Mahabharata in simplicity, but they use extremely incorrect language, and commentators are frequently driven to explain bad forms as 'Arsh.' Nor is their language sublime and dignified. The language of the Mahabharata bears the impress of a writer who is the master of a spoken language. It has been observed by Arnold that Milton, whose language, in spite of its ruggedness, corresponds in dignity with the dignity of the subject, does not use chaste and pure English. He uses Latin and Greek words and even Latin and Greek constructions in English garb. I think the language of the Mahabharata, though not ponderous like the language of the Paradise Lost, compares favourably with it in point of purity.

Whoever wishes to realise the beauty of the language of the Mahabharata should read the Bhagwat Gita, which is indeed what the author has said about it, the nectar and essence of the whole poem. It not only contains the highest philosophy which the Mahabharata has to teach, but it exhibits the author's command over the Sanskrit language in the highest degree. In the whole range of non-vedic Sanskrit literature there is not a single work which can equal the Bhagwat Gita in simplicity of language, in correctness of expression and the deep sonorousness of its period. The words and sentences in this best of songs are indeed cast in pure gold, for they are small in compass, weighty and brilliant.

The epic poem need have no moral. But the Mahabharata has one distinctly. It is the binding cord which runs through the whole of this vast fabric holding fast its several parts. We are not left to guess what this moral is. The author has told it himself in his own words. The observance of Dharma, under any condition or in any adversity, is the duty which the Mahabharata tries constantly to inculcate throughout its length. One may render the word Dharma as our whole duty to God and man. There are four shlokas at the end of the Mahabharata which contain this moral and which are collectively called Bharata-Savitri. It was stated by a Shastri that Bharata-Savitri used to be recited every morning by pious Brahmins as a part of what is called the Pratahsmarana or morning prayer. We shall conclude this piece of criticism with quoting and translating one of these shlokas:—

ऊर्ध्वबाहुर्विरौम्येष न च कश्चिच्छृणोति माम्।
धर्मादर्थश्च कामश्च स धर्मः किं न सेव्यते॥

Rendered into English verse this stands as follows:—

With arms uplifted, loud I cry;
But no one deigns to hear.
Pleasure and wealth from duty flow,
Duty why not revere?

MAHABHARATA AS A HISTORY.

THE MAHABHARATA AS A HISTORY.

CHAPTER I.

The Date of the Mahabharata War.

The Mahabharata war or rather battle is the first authentic event in the ancient history of India. The authenticity of the fight of Rama with the Rakshasa, king of Lanka, has been questioned by many; but nobody has doubted the truth of the event of the terrible battle on the plains of Kurukshetra which ended in the total destruction of two vast armies. When did the fight take place? That is a question on which diverse opinions have been recorded. The earliest date assigned to the Mahabharata war is that fixed by Mr. Modak on the basis of some astronomical data found in the Mahabharata. He thinks that the vernal equinox at the time of the war was in Punarvasu and hence about 7,000 years must have elapsed since then. Some thinkers, following the opinion of Varaha Mihira, believe that the battle was fought in 2604 B.C. European scholars on the other hand believe on the authority of a Shloka in the Vishnu Purana that the war took place about 1500 B.C. Mr. Dutta gives 1250 B.C. as the date of the Kuru-Panchal war on the basis of the Magadha annals which show that thirty-five kings reigned in Magadha between the Kuru-Panchal war and the time of Buddha. Mr. Velandi Ayyar, in a pamphlet only recently published, calculates the exact date of the war or battle as the 14th of October 1194 B.C. The orthodox opinion, however, is that the war took place in 3101 B.C. calculating on the basis of the generally accepted belief in India that in 1899 A.D. five thousand years had elapsed since the beginning of the Kali-age. We agree with this orthodox opinion and will in this chapter discuss the evidence both internal and external (the latter to be divided again into Indian and Foreign) on which we rely.

The Mahabharata war is held among the Aryans of India as synchronous with the beginning of the Kali-age and naturally enough. The Aryans of India had arrived, as we will show in a separate place, at a very high state of both moral and material progress at the time of the war and the war was the beginning of its downfall. Departures from fixed moral rules begun by one party were multiplied by the other in retaliation; so much so that the last unpardonable action of Bhima in breaking the thigh of Duryodhana with his mace[1] was retaliated by Ashwatthama slaughtering innocent men and children at night in sleep. This moral downfall was followed by the annihilation of the material power of both parties and the Aryans in consequence gradually fell, never to recover thereafter their former position, as history has painfully proved. In short, Kali-yuga has

1 Krishna apologising to his enraged brother Balarama for this most unlawful conduct of Bhima can only say प्राप्तं कलियुगं विद्धि प्रतिज्ञा पांडवस्यन्च । गदा. प.

properly been believed to begin with the great war between the Pandavas and the Kauravas.

It is suggested by Talboys Wheeler that Shrikrishna was not in existence at the time of this great war. But the great Krishna cannot be separated from the Pandavas. In fact, the Mahabharata would not have been what it is but for his wonderful personality. We have strong external evidence also in support of this connection. Heracles, who is none other than Krishna, and Pandia have been talked of together by Greek historians, though by similarity of sound the Pandias of the south have undoubtedly been mistaken for the Pandavas.[1] The curious story is related by Greek authors that Heracles had a daughter by name Pandia on whom he raised progeny by incest and assigned to it a country which lies to the south and extends to the sea. (McCrindle's ancient India). Here is a jumble of names and facts. The Pandavas were no doubt the sons of Krishna's father's sister, and his own sister was the mother of the next heir. But the Pandias were a different race of Indians altogether who settled in the south of India and among whom peculiar marriage institutions obtained (probably copied from the native inhabitants), such as the marriage between sisters and brothers. The same story as stated by the Greeks has, I believe, been copied by Feristah in the introduction to his great work wherein he gives a summary of the ancient legendary history of India. To return to our point, even

[1] Weber refers to this fact and the natural inference, but makes light of it. He similarly disposes the Sutra of Panini wherein वासुदेव and अर्जुन are talked of together, page 137.

this mistaken account given by Greek authors shows that so far back as 300 B.C. Shrikrishna and the Pandavas were inseparably connected in the public mind in India.

We may therefore grant that the fixing of the date of the Mahabharata war is the same as the fixing of the date of the beginning of the Kali-age and the date of Shrikrishna. We shall now collect and discuss the evidence bearing on these three points.

In discussing internal evidence we have to bear in mind that the original Mahabharata, as has already been shown in Book I, was at least twice recast, the last time about 300 B.C. It is often difficult to decide whether a particular sentiment, idea or statement of fact in the Mahabharata belongs to the last mentioned period, or to the time of the original nucleus of the Epic. But we shall have to do so and we have already given some general principles on which this can be done with tolerable accuracy. Bearing this in mind we shall first proceed to see what inference as to time can be drawn from the state of society and knowledge described in the original Mahabharata.

The Vedic period is usually divided into two parts, the Mantra period and the Brahmana period. It appears pretty certain that the Mahabharata war took place in the middle of the Brahmana period. Holding, as we do, that the author Vyasa was a contemporary of the event and wrote his poem some time after the war, we may derive some argument from the language of the original poem. The language of Vyasa is simple and forcible, and bears the mark of a spoken language. It is also archaic in appearance and stands on the same level with the language of the Upnishadas. The poet has often a fancy to indulge in the composition of metres after the Vedic fashion though Anushtub has been established on a firm basis as the metre of epic or Puranik poetry. The state of society described is very nearly the same as in the Upnishadas. The Aryans had arrived at a very high state of civilization. Kings, armies, palaces and gardens are spoken of in both. Caste had not become quite exclusive though it was gradually being stratified. Brahmanas had established a character for sanctity and were beginning to be revered as saintly beings who had attained to divine powers. Animal food, even beef, was freely eaten by Kshatriyas and Brahmanas. Sacrifices were the order of the day, though faith in these rituals had begun to be shaken by new principles preached as Sankhya, Yoga and Vedanta. We shall have to discuss this subject at greater length in a separate place; but these salient features are enough to indicate that the Mahabharata war took place about the time when the Brahmanas were being and had partly been composed.

This conclusion is not shaken by what we find from a consideration of external Indian evidence. The Brahmanas contain no direct reference to the great war no doubt, but this is only a negative argument. For there are other indications which show that the war must have taken place about the middle of the Brahmana period. The older portions of the Shatapatha Brahmana speak of the Kurus and Panchalas as two flourishing communities. The later portions have a direct reference to Janmejaya Parikshita and his brothers Shrutasena,

Ugrasena and Bhimasena, the great-grand-sons of Arjuna. These facts would lead us to think that the great war must have taken place in the interval. We have again the direct mention of 'Krishna Devaki Putra' as a teacher of Vedanta in the Chhandoyoga Upnishad. Vyasa lastly is mentioned as a Rishi in one of the Parishishtas of the Kathaka Brahmana of the Black Yajus (Weber, p. 93), though we have no mention of him earlier.

Weber in commenting on the mention of Janmejaya Parikshita in the later portions of the Shatapatha Brahmana observes, "How is this contradiction to be explained. That something great and marvellous had happened in the family of the Parikshitas and that their end still excited astonishment at the time of the Brahmana has already been stated. But what it was we know not. After what has been said above, it can hardly have been the overthrow of the Kurus by the Panchalas; but at any rate it must have been deeds of guilt; and indeed I am inclined to regard this as the yet unknown 'something' which is the basis of the legend of the Mahabharata." (Weber, p. 136). Mr. Dutta, following the train of thought started by Weber, says, "The literature of the times which makes frequent mention of Janmejaya Parikshita has not a word to say about the Pandavas who are entirely unknown to Vedic Sanskrit Literature. Arjuna was still the name of Indra and Indra's Vedic combats with the rain cloud have thus been mixed up with the facts of a historical war! To take one more instance, Janmejaya Parikshita was, according to contemporaneous testimony, himself stained with the guilt of the war. In the modern Epic Janmejaya is the great-grandson of Arjuna who was engaged in war." (Dutta's 1st Edition.)[1]

Here is another instance of a jumble of ideas. What contemporaneous testimony states that Janmejaya was stained with the guilt of the *war?* In fact, the war has not been mentioned at all in the Shatapatha Brahmana. Janmejaya is stated to have incurred the sin of Bramhahatya and not the sin of waging a war. And whence does Weber derive his idea of the astonishing end of the Parikshitas? The Brihadaranya only refers to a question put to Yadnyavalkya by a Gandharva as to where the Parikshitas were. It is a question which may be asked about any person whose end is not marvellous. This is a digression but one necessitated by the mistake which Mr. Dutta has committed of confounding the sin of Bramhahatya with the Mahabharata war.[1] The omission of the mention of the war in the Shatapatha Brahmana is not of great importance as we will show in the next chapter where the whole question is discussed in detail. Since we have the direct mention of Janmejaya Parikshita and of Amba, Ambika and Ambalaya and Subhadra and Arjuna and Falguna and other names familiar in the Bharata therein, we cannot doubt that the war must have taken place in the interval.

It thus seems very probable from internal and external evidence that the Mahabharata war took place after the Shatapatha Brahman had been commenced, and certainly before the later portions of it, and some of the oldest Upnishadas, such as Chhandoyoga and Brihadaranya,

1 In the Second Edition of Dutta's Ancient Civilization of India these ideas and inferences have been dropped.

were composed. This by itself does not lead us to any definite conclusions as to its date. But the time may still be approximately determined. Although European scholars have generally assigned to the Vedas a very late date, later researches, especially those of Mr. Tilak and Shankar Dixit, have shown that the Mantra portion of the Vedas was composed at least about 4,000 years before the Christian Era and that the Brahmanas were probably composed about 3,000 B.C. We do not wish here to capitulate the arguments of Dixit which relate to the date of the Mantra portion of the Vedas. We are only concerned with his arguments relating to the date of the composition of the Brahmanas. These arguments of Dixit are, in our opinion, very strong and do not admit of any controversy. Dixit's work "The History of Bharatiya Jyotish Shastra" has not, we believe, been translated into English, and we take the liberty of giving below his chief arguments. In the Shatapatha Brahmana, K. 2, it is said 'Etaha vai prachyai dishona chyavante, Sarvani ha va anyani nakshatrani prachyai dishashchyavanti.' "These (the Krittika) do not swerve from the east, while all other Nakshatras do." This clearly proves that in the days of the Shatapatha Brahmana, Kand II, the Krittikas rose exactly in the east and must, therefore, have been on the celestial equator. This must have been according to Dixit's calculation about 3,000 years or more before the Christian Era. And if we remember the roughness of Vedic observations we shall have to allow a margin of two or even three centuries to the time above calculated. So far as we have been able to ascertain there seems no reason why the date fixed by Dixit within a variation of one or two centuries should not be taken to be the date of the composition of the older portions of the Shatapatha Brahmana. The Bharata war happened some time after this and before the later portions of the Brahmana were composed. These later portions must have been composed long before the Vedanga Jyotisha, the date of which from the astronomical observations recorded therein appears to be about 1500 B.C. (*see* Dixit) and they may safely be assigned to about 2000 B.C. at the latest. The Mahabharata war must thus have been fought between 3100 B.C. and 2000 B.C.

The rising of the Krittikas exactly in the east referred to in the Shatapatha Brahmana, Kanda II, has furnished us with a reliable basis for fixing the date of that portion of the Brahmana. That the Mahabharata war took place soon after this, can be inferred from the almost unanimous testimony of Indian astronomers. As has already been stated, the Mahabharata war has always been looked upon as the beginning of the Kali-age and Indian astronomers have generally accepted and expressed the same view. The Mahabharata itself preaches and maintains this idea, as will appear from the various quotations given below :—

Antare chaiva samprapte Kalidvaparayorabhut, Syamantapanchake yuddham Kurupandavasenayoh ; Adi Parva.

Praptam Kaliyugam Viddhi pratijna Pandavasya cha, Gada Parva.

Etatkaliyugam nama achiradyat pravartate ; Vana Parva.

The same idea has been expressed by the astronomical Siddhantas, which probably date from the first century of the Christian Era, by the first Arya-bhatta who preceded Varaha Mihira and flourished about 450 A.D. and lastly by the Indian astronomers who lived after him down to the present day. Taking 300 B.C. as the date of the recasting of the Mahabharata as we have it, we find that from 300 B.C. down to the present day, the belief in India has been that the Mahabharata war took place about the beginning of the Kali-age.[1] Now all the Indian astronomers agree in stating that the Kali-age began in 3101 B.C. It follows naturally that in the opinion of the Indian astronomers, who range from 100 A.D., the Mahabharata war took place about 3101 B.C.

Whence did the Indian astronomers derive that date for the beginning of the Kali-age? That is a question which has puzzled many thinkers and Dixit himself is one of them. It is suggested by him that the astronomers perhaps obtained that date by calculation. They supposed that the beginning of the Kali-age was marked by the coming of the planets near Ashwini and found the year 3101 B.C. as the one which most nearly fulfilled that condition. But there is no authority to hold that the Indian astronomers thought that the beginning of the Kali-age was marked by the coming together of the planets near Ashwini. Nor does it appear that the real positions of the planets were near Ashwini in the year 3101 B.C. Dixit takes Madhyama Grahas or their mean positions and bases his theory upon them. But Madhyama Grahas are of no use in this connection, as the Spashta or real positions of the planets often differ by very large amounts from their Madhyama or

1 The Surya-siddhanta speaks of Bharata as interchangeable with the beginning of the Kali-age when it speaks of Bharata Guru, *see* Dixit, p. 193.

mean positions. In fine, this theory of a fictitious beginning being obtained by calculation fails because the two premises on which it rests are themselves untrue.

It appears very probable that the date of the beginning of the Kali-age, assigned by the Indian astronomers, was obtained by tradition in the same manner as the Mahabharata war has been by tradition identified with that beginning. We have come across a very strong piece of external evidence in support of this view. The Greek historians of India, who derived their information about this country at the time of Alexander and also from the now unfortunately lost work of Megasthenes, have recorded the following about the chronological beliefs which prevailed in those days in India. "From the time of Dionysos to Sandrakottos, the Indians counted 153 kings, and a period of 6,042 years. But among these a republic was thrice established. The Indians also tell us that Dionysos was earlier than Heracles by 15 generations" (McCrindle's Ancient India, p. 204). Now although there may be a doubt as to who this Dionysos was, it is admitted on all hands that Heracles was no other than Hari or Shrikrishna. "This Heracles is held in special honour by the Shourseni Indian tribe who possess two large cities, Mathora and Cleisobora. It is further said that he had a very numerous progeny (for, like his Theban namesake he married many wives)."—(Ditto, p. 201.) This description of Heracles should, we think, be enough to identify him with Shrikrishna, the contemporary of the Pandavas. Since there were 153 generations from

Dionysos to Chandragupta and Dionysos was 15 generations earlier than Heracles it follows that Heracles preceded Chandragupta by 138 generations of kings. Taking 20 years as the average for each reign, we have an approximate period of 2,760 years separating the two. Chandragupta's date is 312 B.C. which gives us 3072 B.C. as the approximate date of Shrikrishna. It very nearly tallies with the date of the Mahabharata war given by Indian astronomers.

Such was the tradition prevalent in India in 312 B.C., *i.e.*, at a time when European scholars are agreed that the Indians had not learnt or discovered the methods of calculating the positions of planets. That the inquisitive Greek ambassador at the court of Chandragupta has left carefully sifted information about India without exaggeration or fabrication has also been admitted.[1] The only possible way in which the above tradition may be impeached is by supposing that the Indians themselves had exaggerated notions about their antiquity. This agrument, however, is not of much value as we have arrived at our figure by taking the generally accepted average of 20 years for each reign. It cannot be argued that even the number of generations has been exaggerated. The charge has often been brought against the Indians that they had no idea of history. I think that the charge has been lightly made. Works known as histories or Itihasas were known even in Vedic times. The Mahabharata itself was originally a history. Historical facts, especially genealogies, were most carefully recorded at all times in ancient India.

[1] See Hunter's Indian Empire.

The detailed figures given by Megasthenes himself clearly prove that this was done in his time. Houen Tsang has recorded it as a fact that annals were carefully recorded in each State. The Rajatarangini speaks of ancient histories of Kashmere. In the presence of such evidence extending over such a long period we cannot believe that history had no existence in India. Even now Rajput genealogies and even the genealogies of Banias and Mewatis are recorded very carefully by Bhatas who gain their living by this profession alone. It was, we believe only once, *viz.*, between 700 and 1000 A.D. when Buddhism was overthrown and modern Hinduism established, that historical darkness came upon the land and most of the ancient annals were either destroyed or tampered with. The evidence which we have adduced from Greek sources does not belong to this period but is as old as 312 B.C. and cannot be looked upon as exaggerated or tampered with. Even granting all that can be urged against us, this much at least cannot be gainsaid, *viz.*, that the idea that the Mahabharata war took place about 3100 B.C. is as old as Megasthenes.

We are now in a position to consider the contradictory evidence adduced from the Vishnu Purana and the Bhagavata which presumably follows the former in this respect. We will use Mr. Dutta's translation of the Vishnu Purana here. In the last section of Part IV Parashara says, "From the birth of king Parikshita up to the installation of king Nanda, it is to be known that 1065 years have passed." This, no doubt, would give to the Mahabharata war a date much later than we have assigned, *viz.*, somewhere about 1400 B.C. But this statement in the Vishnu Purana is opposed to what has been stated in it a little before. The Vishnu Purana purports to have been recited when Parikshita was ruling the earth (*see* the last sentence of Section 20). At the end of Section 23 it is stated that kings of the Brihadratha race will rule in Magadha for 1,000 years.[1] Then follows the Pradyota dynasty, of which it is predicted, "these five kings of the Pradyota race shall govern the earth for 138 years" (Section 24). Then follow kings of the Shishunaga race "who will lord over the earth for 362 years." Hereafter comes the Shudra king, Mahapadmananda, with his 8 sons, who will rule the earth for 100 years. Now adding up the periods of kings before Nanda we find—

Brihadratha dynasty	1,000 years.
Pradyota dynasty	138 ,,
Shishunaga dynasty	362 ,,
	1,500 years.

The Brihadratha dynasty is counted from Sahadeva, son of Jarasandha, killed by Bhima, and contemporary of the Mahabharata war. How can the statement of 1,065 years, then, be reconciled with this? Then again we have the following statement immediately after the former :—" At the birth of the king Parikshita they (the Saptarishis) were in Magha and then the Kali-age began which consists of 1,200 divine years." It is thus admitted by the Vishnu Purana also that the

[1] A round figure like this is generally suspicious.

Kali-age began at the end of the Mahabharata war. It is therefore making a statement opposed to all the astronomers of India when it gives the interval between the war and the reign of Nanda as 1,065 years only. We further find that this length of 1,200 divine years is said to equal 360 800 human years, which is evidently a mistake. In our opinion the statements in the Vishnu Purana are not of much worth. The Purana must have been recast during the revival of Hinduism at the hands of illiterate men; we know what value is usually attached to Puranika geography and astronomy; and we do not think a better value can be attached to Puranik chronology.[1] Especially when we find that it is opposed not only to the evidence of Indian astronomers but also to the evidence of Greek historians who have recorded the traditions prevalent in India in 300 B.C., we cannot but regard this conflicting statement in the Vishnu Purana as of little value.

The apparently contradictory statement of Varaha Mihira has next to be considered. The following shloka appears in his Brihatsamhita and is said by him to have been quoted from Garga :—

> "Asanmaghasu munayah shasati Prithivim Yudhisthire Nripatau.
> Shad dwika panchadwiyutah shakakalah tasya rajnashcha."

[1] Weber observes, "Those works that have come down to us under the name of Puranas are all later productions and belong all of them to the last thousand years or so. They likewise advert in a prophetic tone to the historic line of kings. Here, however, they come into the most violent conflict not only with each other but with chronology in general, so that their historical value in this respect is extremely small." (pp. 190, 191.)

This is generally translated as follows:—The Munis (the Saptarishis) were in Magha when king Yudhisthira ruled the earth. And 2526 when added to Shakakala is the date of that king." This would mean, therefore, that the great king peceded the Shaka Era by 2526 years and not by 3,179 years as is generally believed. Varaha Mihira is thus supposed to assign to the Bharata war a date later by 653 years. It is impossible to believe that Varaha Mihira could have differed from Arya-bhatta who preceded him in this one respect alone; for he agrees with all the other astronomers of India in giving 3101 B.C. as the date of the beginning of the Kali-age. That he should have believed the Bharata war to have been fought 653 years after that beginning, is evidently very strange; and we are naturally led to suspect that the verse quoted above means something else than what it apparently does. A little reflection will show us that this must be so. The verse is quoted from Garga, who is generally believed to have lived before the Christian Era. The word Shakakala used by Garga cannot therefore refer to Shaliwahan Shakabda which was not even born in the days of Garga; some other Shaka is unquestionably referred to by Garga. Mr. Ayyar in his recently published pamphlet has pointed out this fact and believes that the Nirvana Era which was the only one current in Garga's days is referred to in the Shloka. The ingenious interpretation which he puts on 'Shaddwika panchadwi' to suit his own theory cannot, however, be accepted. We think the compound means 2566 and not 2526, the component word 'dwika' meaning 'twice' and not two, the whole word being interpreted according to grammatical rules, as six twice five two. This, when added to the Nirvana Era 543, gives us 3109 B.C., a difference of only 8 years on the generally accepted date of the Yudhishthira Era. What Garga intended by Shaka Kala cannot be definitely determined, but nobody can dispute the fact that the word in Garga's mouth cannot mean the Shalivahana Shaka. Although, therefore, we have not been able to reduce the verse to the exact figure, this much is certain that the discrepancy on which so much stress is laid does not exist and that Varaha Mihira did not assign to Yudhishthira so late a date as 2526+78=2604 B.C.

It is only a few years back that the date of Garga was determined and we now know that he lived about 154 B.C. Kalhana, the author of the Rajatarangini, who lived in the 11th Century A.D., did not probably know it and he naturally interpreted the above oft-quoted verse of Garga in the same manner as has hitherto been done. Kalhana was further confronted by the difficulty of reconciling the generally accepted chronology of the ancient kings of Kashmere with the belief that Gonand, the first king, was a contemporary of the Pandavas, for the total of the years for all the kings did not run up to the traditionally accepted date of the war, in other words the date of the beginning of the Kali-age. Kalhana was, therefore, glad to take his stand on this verse of Garga and to maintain that the tradition which made the Mahabharata war coincide with the beginning of the Kali-age was mistaken. He thought, on the authority of this verse, that the war took place

653 years after the Kali-age had begun and explained the chronology of Kashmere kings accordingly. Kalhana says, (Rajatarangini, Chapter I) "Misled by the tradition that the Bharata war took place at the end of Dwapara, some have doubted the truth of this number of years (given for Kashmere kings). But the Kauravas and Pandavas in reality flourished when six hundred and fifty-three years of the Kali-age had gone." Kalhana then quotes as authority for his statement the well-known Shloka of Garga explained above.

Now that the verse of Garga has been differently interpreted, the difficulty or discrepancy which confronted Kalhana again confronts us. The true solution seems to us to be that Gonand I was not a contemporary of the Pandavas at all as was doubted even in Kalhana's time. The ambition of ancient dynasties in India has generally been to connect themselves by hook or crook with the heroes of the Mahabharata or of the Ramayana, the national epics of India. When Rajput Princes trace their descent from Rama's sons or from Shrikrishna we have a tinge of suspicion that they are drawing more upon their imagination than on solid facts. A similar feeling must have influenced Kashmere historians, and Kalhaṇa among them, when they made Gonand I a contemporary of the Pandavas. We find some support for this argument in the fact that no king of Kashmere is mentioned or noticed in the Mahabharata itself. We have gone over the various Tirtha Yatras and the conquest of the four quarters and the list of the kings engaged in the war; but we have not found any mention of Kashmere kings.[1] If, therefore, we treat Gonanda's being a contemporary of the Pandavas, as itself a mistake, the difficulty which confronted Kalhana disappears and Rajatarangini or the history of Kashmere does not in reality conflict with the view above propounded. Kalhana himself admits that in his days too the tradition was that the Kaliyuga began with the end of the Mahabharata war. The same tradition prevailed in the days of the well-known astronomer Arya-bhatta; the same belief was held in 153 B.C. by Garga himself on whose verse Kalhana raises this controversy; and we have shown that the same tradition prevailed at the time when the Mahabharata was last recast, about 300 B.C. We think the evidence is so strong on this point that we cannot disconnect the two events. One may assign to the beginning of the Kali-age and the war a date later than 3101 B.C, but it cannot be held that the latter happened 653 years after the former.

We now turn to the argument based upon the astronomical references in the Mahabharata of which much has been made by some thinkers. We, on our part, believe that most of these references are of doubtful authenticity, in other words that they do not belong to the original Mahabharata of Vyasa but to its latest edition. It will be admitted by all that some of them are fanciful and absurd. The last editor probably wished to accumulate the number of the evil omens which

[1] Kalhana himself states further on that Gonand being killed in a fight with Krishna, his son being an infant was not asked to take share in the fight between the Kauravas and Pandavas.

preceded the war and tried to put in such impossible combinations as he could bring together. For instance we may safely put aside as absurdities the statement that the sun and the moon were eclipsed at the same time [Chandradityawubhau grastau ekanha hi trayodashim (Bhishma parva)] or the statement that Arundhati went before Vasishtha among the Saptarishis. These may be classed with absurdities in the animal world mentioned further on such as the birth of a cow from a mare or a jackal from a dog (Govatsam vadava sute shwa shrigalam Mahipate, &c.). Rejecting these we come to the mention of the planets occupying or oppressing two sets of constellations or Nakshatras on which principally this theory is based. In the days of the original Bharata the planets were probably not known, and even if they were, their progress along the several constellations could not have been marked. The progress of the moon and the sun was no doubt known and chalked out. It was in fact the basis of the measurement of time. We usually find in old works, even down to the Buddhistic Tripitikas, events marked by a reference to the position of the moon among the constellations. Such observations as the following made by Balaram are typical of these days. 'Pushyena sampra yatosmi shravane punaragataḥ (Gadaparva.)' We will, however, try to explain to the reader how Modaka and his followers argue their date from the double positions of the planets, doubtful as they are, mentioned in the Mahabharata as we have it at the present day and we will show how far their theory is sound.

The following diagram which gives the 27 constellations will be useful for the better understanding of this subject :—

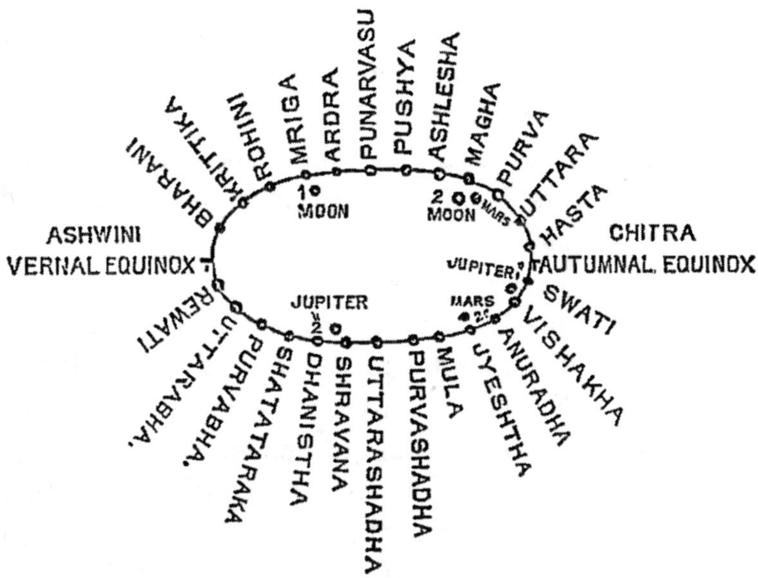

The double positions of the Moon, Mars and Jupiter mentioned in the Mahabharata are as follows :—

In 'Maghavishayagah somah taddinam pratyapadyata.' [1] The Moon is said to be in Magha while she appears to be in Mriga at the beginning of the war from Balaram's statement (' Pushyena samprayatosmi shravane punaragatah,' Gada P.). Mars again is said to be in Magha (Maghaswangarako vakrah, Bhishma P.) as well as in Jyeshtha (Kritwa changarako vakram Jyeshthayam Madhusudana, Udyodga P).[2] Jupiter is said to be in Shravana (Shravanecha Brihaspatih, Bhishma P.) as well

[1] मघा विषयगः सोमस्तद्दिनं प्रत्यपद्यत । भीष्मपर्व.

[2] मघास्वंगारको वक्रः । भीष्म पर्व. कृत्वा चांगारको वक्रं ज्येष्ठायां मधुसूदनां । उद्योग पर्व.

as in Vishakha (Vishakhayah samipasthau Brihaspati shanaishcharau).[1] These double or supposed double positions are sought to be explained by what are called the Sayana and the Nirayana Nakshatras. It is alleged that two sets of Nakshatras were prevalent in those days and ought always to be accepted. As the vernal equinox recedes back among the constellations owing to the precession of the equinoxes we cannot stick to these fixed stars alone. The vernal equinox may be supposed to be the beginning of a set of conventional Nakshatras called Sayana, the first Nakshatra in this conventional set being called Ashwini. For example when the vernal equinox was in the real Nakshatra Mriga, it was the Ashwini Nakshatra in the conventional set and each succeeding Nakshatra changed its name accordingly. When both sets of Nakshatras are mentioned together which Nakshatra is to be taken as the conventional and which the real one, will depend upon the skill of the interpreter. The double positions of the planets mentioned in the Mahabharata are explained by taking the vernal equinox in Punarvasu which in the conventional set will be Ashwini. It is thus explained that the Mriga, Magha and Jyeshtha positions of the Moon, Mars and Jupiter are conventional or Sayana while the Magha, Jyeshtha and Shravana positions are real. These double positions thus indicate, it is said, *only approximately*, that the vernal equinox was situate near Punarvasu at the time of the Bharata war; and this fact can show us how many years have passed since then; the vernal equinox receding nearly one degree in 72 years. Cal-

[1] श्रवणे च बृहस्पतिः। भीष्मपर्व ; विशाखायाः समीपस्थौ बृहस्पतिशनैश्चरौ॥ उद्योगपर्व.

culating on this basis, *viz.*, that the vernal equinox was at the time of the war near Punarvasu, *i.e.*, about 95 degrees behind where it is now, Modaka finds that about 7,000 years must have elapsed since then.

We think that the absurdity of these positions (or rather of these interpretations of shlokas) is only equalled by the absurdity of their explanation. Not only does this theory not suffice to explain accurately all the positions mentioned in the Mahabharata but it is also historically unsound. It takes for granted that the precession of the equinoxes was a thing known in the days of the Mahabharata though as a matter of fact we know that the Greeks discovered this precession only a little before the Christian Era and in India even Varaha Mihira, who lived about 500 A.D., did not know it.[1] It also takes for granted that the Nakshatras always began with Ashwini though we have evidence in the Brahmanas, the Vedang Jyotisha and the Mahabharata itself that down to 100 A.D. they always began with Krittikas. The confusion which would necessarily be caused by having two sets of Nakshatras, one conventional and the other real, possessing the same names without any distinction as to their nature, has been admitted by these theorists themselves. It would require an ingenious eye every time to detect the nature of the constellation mentioned and ancient sages were probably not fond of introducing such confusion in names, well aware that ingenious men are always few and far between and they

1 *See* his well-known shloka about the position of the संपात in his time.

would certainly have added some epithet to mark the conventional Nakshatras.

The different positions mentioned in the Mahabharata are no doubt difficult to explain. Perhaps Sauti, the last editor of the Mahabharata who inserted hundreds of Kuta shlokas in it, intended some of his shlokas to be astronomical riddles and the commentator of the Mahabharata does treat the shloka 'Maghavishayagah somastaddinam pratyapadyata' as a kind of riddle. He has solved it by showing that 'Maghavishayagah' meant that the moon was in the Pitriloka, *i.e.*, it was really in Mriga. The word 'Vishaya' lends great support to this interpretation. If the shlokas are carefully interpreted many of these apparent discrepancies disappear, especially if we interpret the word 'pidayan' (oppressing) as meaning only oppressing by 'Vedha' or 'Drishti' as it is called, either direct, *i.e.*, in opposition or traingular as the commentator has done. It would be uninteresting to the general reader to enter into the examination of each passage here and we leave the subject to be dealt with in the Appendix (*see* note V).

It now remains to consider the opinion of Mr. Dutta and Mr. Ayyar. The Magadha annals on which the former bases his date are, I believe, the same as the Puranik accounts of which we have spoken before and he himself has admitted the untrustworthiness of the Puranika annals (p. 30, Vol. II). These, therefore, require no separate notice and we proceed to notice the ingenious theory which Mr. Ayyar has propounded in his recently published book. From what has already been stated it will appear that Mr. Ayyar has only partially used the materials available in the Greek accounts of India. He has tried with great difficulty to identify Dionysos with Ikshwaku and has entirely ignored Heracles whose identification with Hari or Shrikrishna is so apparent. He has also tried to make profit out of Garga's statement "that after the destruction of the Greeks at the end of the Yuga seven powerful kings will reign in Oudh," and maintains that the Kali-age, which even Garga admits, began with the Mahabharata war, was to last for only a thousand years and ended with the expulsion of the Greeks from India in about 150 B.C. It cannot be believed that Indian astronomers, who have always taken 1,200 divine years as the duration of the Kali-age (a divine day being equal to an ordinary year), ever believed that the Kali-age was only to last for 1,000 human years. The ingenious meaning which Mr. Ayyar has assigned to the famous shloka of Varaha Mihira 'Shaddwika Pachadwiyutah' cannot be accepted and was not known to Kalhana. We have indicated above the chief points where Mr. Ayyar's theory seems to be pregnable and the limits of this work do not allow us to enter into a detailed discussion of his arguments.

To take a resume : the Mahabharata war has always been taken in India at least from 300 B.C. as the begining of the Kali-age and Shrikrishna is a central figure of the war. The fixing of the date of the Mahabharata war, therefore, is the same as fixing the date of Shrikrishna and the beginning of the Kali-age. The Mahabharata war appears to have been fought when the Shatapatha Brahmana was being composed. From

Shatapatha Brahmana, Kand II, it appears that when these earlier portions of the Brahmana were composed the constellation of the Krittikas always rose in the east, a thing which according to Dixit's calculation used to happen about 3000 B.C. We may thus assign to the composition of the Shatapatha Brahmana, Kand II, a date between 3000 to 3200 B.C. taking into consideration the roughness of Vedic observations. The war was the beginning of the Kali-age to which the Indian astronomers have assigned 3101 B.C. by tradition. For the evidence of the Greek historians of India who have given the chronology of kings, as was then believed in, in India, shows that Heracles who is none else than Shrikrishna was removed from Sandrakottos or Chandragupta by 137 generations, and taking 20 years for each generation as an average, must thus be supposed to have lived 2,740 years before Chandragupta, *i.e.*, about 3052 B.C. The Puranik annals which contradict this chronology are of very little historical value. These Puranas were recast about 800 A.D. by illiterate persons who probably did not know when Nanda lived and whose testimony, opposed as it is to Greek historians and all the Indian astronomers, is of no value. The date currently assigned to the Mahabharata war appears, therefore, to be the proper one and is one which has been assigned at least from 300 B.C. downwards. The contradictory theory of Modaka is not based on strong grounds while that of Mr. Ayyar omits to take into account Heracles whose identification with Krishna is so palpable. It may perhaps be said that in accepting the orthodox date assigned to the Mahabharata war we are going too far back into the hoary vista of antiquity. But if we look at the dates which modern researches have established in connection with events in the histories of Egypt, Babylonia and China, it will appear that the date assigned to the first authentic event in the history of ancient India is not incredible. It is believed that the highest pyramid of Egypt, which still survives and is one of the 7 wonders of the world, was built about 2500 B.C. and this presages a high state of civilization and a settled form of government existing from several centuries earlier.[1] Babylonian history goes so far back as 2458 B.C. and when it is admitted that civilization in Babylonia came from districts lower down, "the beginnings of civilization in these districts may be placed not below than 3000 B.C." In China native historians go far still further back, but it is admitted that the historical king Hangtwi came to the throne in 2332 B.C. His predecessor, it is said, taught agriculture to his people, established public markets and discovered the medical properties of herbs. Genealogies of kings again with accurate information about the duration of reigns, with the exception of exaggerated figures for a few kings in the beginning, were preserved in Egyptian temples when Herodotus visited them. Again Hebrew genealogies of Patriarchs of quite a similar character are still preserved in the scriptures of these people and Chinese genealogies similarly are still

1 "If, therefore, we assume that the pyramids were built about the year 2500 B.C. the beginning of higher civilization in the valley of the Nile cannot be placed later than 3000 B.C."—(History of Antiquity by Prof. Max. Danker, Vol. 1, p. 34.)

given in the histories written by Chinamen. It need not be wondered, therefore, that genealogies of kings with accurate figures for the several reigns, except perhaps for the kings in the beginning, were extant in the days of Megasthenes. In fine, it is not at all strange that the historical memories of the Indian Aryans, like those of the other great nations of antiquity, go so far back as 3101 B.C.[1]

[1] In this connection we may bear in mind the fact that the products of the Indus and the Ganges (including the well-known silks of India) were brought by the ships of the Indians to Arabia about 2000 B. C." —*See* Ditto p. 322.)

CHAPTER II.

WERE THE PANDAVAS REAL BEINGS?

HAVING in the previous chapter disposed of the controversy as to the date of the great war between the two kindred Aryan tribes, the Kurus and the Panchalas, we will now proceed to discuss the controversy as to the actors in the great struggle. It has generally been conceded that the Mahabharata has "as a historical background an ancient conflict between two neighbouring tribes who finally coalesced into a single people." The most diverse opinions have, however, been held not only as to when this conflict took place but also as to who were the parties to it. Mr. Dutta following the arguments advanced by Weber and others believes that "the Pandavas must be set down as mythical heroes," because there is no mention of them in contemporary Vedic literature, while other personages who figure in the Mahabharata war are frequently met with. For example Janmejaya, the son of Parikshita, is often mentioned, though Arjuna his great-grandfather and chief hero of the Bharata war is conspicuous by his absence. Arjuna is still the name of Indra in the Brahmanas. Before, therefore, we go on to give a historical sketch of the events which form the subject of narration in the great epic we must discuss the question whether the Pandavas were real or imaginary beings.

Generally speaking, the mention of a person or an event in a work which professes to be a history is sufficient evidence of the fact that such a person existed or that such an event happened. To prove the existence of Moses or Romulus no other evidence is required or can be forthcoming, except histories or the traditions on which such histories as cannot always have been written by contemporary persons, rest. Of course the evidence of tradition and of history may be rejected if rebutted by other evidence or if they are shown to be untrusworthy for cogent reasons. *Prima facie* we may take it therefore, that the Pandavas and their opponents lived and acted as described in the Mahabharata which professes to be a history and not a novel, unless we are given strong arguments to the contrary.

The negative argument which is often used to disparage these presumptions is sometimes used without much consideration. The absence of the mention of the Pandavas in contemporaneous or later Vedic literature, if we devote a little thought to the subject, would be of no import whatever, unless it was further shown that their mention therein was necessary. To take an extreme illustration hundreds of books were written at the time of the battle of Par-de-burgh and have been written since. But most of them contain no mention whatever of Lord Roberts or Lord Kitchener, undoubtedly the greatest heroes of the present day; nor even of the battle. It will be quite illogical to argue that because these books make no mention of Lord Roberts or Lord Kitchener these men never existed. Since the great battle of Panipat which was fought between the Marahtas and the Afgans many books and poems, both in Marathi and English, have been written. It is absurd to expect in every one of them a reference to that battle or to the leaders in it. Nobody would be justified in holding, that because one does not find any mention of Sadashiva Rao Bhau or of Jankoji Scindia in a particular book written after the battle of Panipat, no such beings therefore ever existed. These concrete illustrations though extreme, are enough to show the absurdity of the negative argument. It would be different if the books referred to above were histories of the Boers or the Marahtas written at the time of these events or subsequently. For such histories must in the ordinary course contain a mention of these events and the persons who took part in them. Now it is well-known that Vedic Literature is generally concerned with the explanations of ceremonies and some times of philosophical and theological dogmas. Historical references come in very rarely and that too by way of illustration. It would be impossible to suppose that Vedic works would mention by way of illustration every event that had happened or every person who had lived. In our opinion their silence about the great war or about the Pandavas cannot logically be construed into a disproof of them; for the historical evidence we have in the Mahabharata has not been impeached on valid grounds.

There are, however further strong grounds why the theory that the Pandavas were imaginary beings cannot be accepted. In the original edition of his book Mr. Dutta expressed his belief that while the war was really fought the Pandavas were poetical additions subsequently made, being the ideal personifications of certain moral excellencies. Several incidents in the life of the Pandavas related in the Mahabharata, however, do not fit in with this theory. For instance, the five brothers are related to have married one and the same woman. Now polygamy was not practised or rather countenanced by the Aryans of India at any time. The Vedic Rishis said "as one sacrificial cord cannot go round many sacrificial posts one woman cannot marry many men," though one man, in their opinion, could marry more than one woman as many sacrificial cords could be tied round one post. How then were these later personifications of virtue represented to have done an act entirely opposed to Aryan notions of good behaviour? Even the Mahabharata itself admits the unusual character of this proceeding and we plainly see in the Epic different attempts made at different times to explain this seemingly inconsistent conduct of its heroes. Again Bhima is said to have drunk the blood of Duhshasana when he killed him in battle in order to mark the revenge he had taken on him for his dastardly action in ill-treating Draupadi. This barbarous act too is offensive to the sense of right conduct in every man and cannot be supposed to have been predicated of ideal heroes conceived in later times. In fact the Mahabharata here also makes an attempt in a subsequent chapter, evidently an interpolation of later days, to exculpate Bhima by stating that Bhima only made a show of drinking the blood and did not actually drink it. These and other minor actions to our mind show that the Pandavas were real beings and not imaginary heroes. It may perhaps be urged that these conceptions belong to a time when polygamy may have been practised by the Aryans of India or the drinking of human blood was not repugnant to their ideas. If we grant that this was the case, of which there is great doubt, it will be conceded that this must have been so at a very ancient date indeed. This supposition, therefore, if not tantamount to the admission that the Pandavas were real beings, is at least not better.

One may still be tempted to urge that the absence of the mention in later Vedic Literature of the heroes of such a vast and all-engrossing Epic as the Mahabharata is at least very suspicious if not positively harmful. To them our answer is that the Mahabharata, as shown in the first book, was not then what it now is. It was then only one of the many floating Itihasas or episodes mentioned in the Brahmana Literature as a subject of study. It was not that comprehensive work which Sauti has made it nor had the incidents of the war been invested with that religious or mythological halo which is their engrossing charm in the present Epic. For Krishna worship was still an infant creed when the Brahmanas were composed and had not reached those dimensions which we find it had assumed in the days of Megasthenes. It is therefore quite compatible with the possibilities of nature that the historical incidents of the great war, not yet exaggerated nor associated with religious ideas, were not referred to by way of illustration by the Brahmanic Rishis. Lastly, the great war itself is nowhere referred to in the Brahmanas. If then in spite of the absence of its mention in the Brahmanas the truth of the great war has been conceded on all hands, one fails to see why the absence of the mention of its heroes should be taken to prove that they alone were not real but mythical.

We now pass on to the second issue, *viz.*, whether Janmejaya was the person who was really engaged in the Mahabharata fight. This has been a little anticipated in a previous chapter, but it would not be much amiss if the whole subject is here brought together as in a focus. Weber thinks that there is a great confusion in the Mahabharata as to who this Janmejaya was. He is sometimes represented as an ancestor. He is again said to be a son of Parikśhita, the grandson of Arjuna. A Janmejaya Parikshita is mentioned in the 13th Kanda of the Shatapatha Brahmana, where it is related that he performed a horse-sacrifice with the help of the sage Indrota Devapi Shaunaka and was thereby absolved wholly from the sin of Brahmahatya. It is therefore inferred that there was only one Janmejaya, the great-grandson of Arjuna, and that the sin or guilt of which he was absolved was the sin of the great war.

It is no doubt true that there is some confusion in the Mahabharata as to whether Parikshita Janmejaya was an ancestor or a descendant of the great heroes of the Mahabharata war. The confusion, or rather contradiction, is due to the attempt of the last editor of the Mahabharata, as has been shown in the first book, to increase the bulk of the Bharata of Vaishampayana by repetition as well as by the bringing in of all the floating minor historical episodes which were current in his days. In the Adi-Parva, Chapter 94, we have a genealogy of the Pandavas given in metre, while in the very next chapter, which is in prose, the same has been given again. It seems probable that the metrical Chapter 94 is a subsequent addition by Sauti as has already been remarked.

For the two genealogies, differing from each other, give the descendants from Kuru to Shantanu as follows :—

CHAPTER 94.

- Kuru.
  - Avikshita Janmejaya.
    - Parikshita.
      - Janmejaya.
        - Dhritarashtra.
          - Pratipa.
            - Devapi.
            - Shantanava.
            - Balhika.
          - and others.
        - Pandu.
        - Balhika.
        - 5 others.
      - Kukshasena.
        - Indrasena.
      - Ugrasena.
        - Sushena.
      - Chandrasena.
        - Bhimasena.
    - 7 other-sons.

CHAPTER 95.

- Kuru.
  - Vidura.
    - Anashwa.
      - Parikshita.
        - Bhimasena.
          - Pratishrava.
            - Pratipa.
              - Devapi.
              - Shantanu.
              - Balhika.

It is plain from Chapter 95 that there was a Janmejaya but not a Parikshita Janmejaya among the ancestors of the Pandavas. It is possible to reply that Parikshita may have had, besides Bhimasena, other sons, one of whom may have been Janmejaya. This supposition, it may further be urged, is strengthened by the fact that in Chapter 150 of the Shantiparva Bhishma relates to Yudhishthira how Janmejaya Parikshita was purified from the sin of Brahmahatya by the help of Indrota Devapi Shaunaka. The Janmejaya Parikshita therein mentioned must necessarily have been an ancestor of both Bhishma and Yudhishthira. It seems, however, that this chapter has also been added subsequently by Sauti in order to collate the Vedic legend given in the Shaṭapatha Brahmana and in consequence of this addition he had to make some alterations in the genealogy as given in Chapter 94. For Janmejaya is presumably the eldest of all the brothers in this chapter as well as in Vedic legend, while in Chapter 95, if Bhimasena had any brother by name Janmejaya, he must be supposed to have been a younger brother. as Bhimasena would not otherwise have been the representative of the family of Parikshita. Recurrence of names is met with in all genealogies, whether ancient or modern, Eastern or European. The device adopted in modern histories to distinguish kings bearing the same name is to add their number. We distinguish kings of England as Edward I or Edward II or the Emperors of Dehli as Akabar I or Akabar II. The device adopted in the Vedic Literature appears to have been to add the name of the father or the mother. The

Rishis are always spoken of as Baka Dalbhya, Ushasti Chakrayana and kings as Harishchandra Aikshwaka or Janmejaya Parikshita. The genealogy given in the prose Chapter 95, gives a Janmejaya and also a Parikshita among the ancestors of the Pandavas, but that Janmejaya was not the son of Parikshita. It seems more probable that there was only one Janmejaya Parikshita than that there were two, one an ancestor and the other a descendant of the Pandavas. All these arguments go to support the idea that Sauti has interpolated the genealogical Chapter 94 in verse in the Adiparva as also the legend of Janmejaya Parikshita and Devapi Shaunaka from the Shatapatha Brahmana in Chapter 150 of the Shantiparva. There is another mention of Janmejaya Parikshita in the Mahabharata in Adiparva, Chapter 2, from which can be derived additional support to the above idea. There we have, as in the Shatapatha Brahmana, the four brothers, Janmejaya, Shrutasena, Ugrasena and Bhimasena, mentioned together, and the word Papakritya is also used there. This probably shows that here too we have the same Shatapatha legend and the chapter being in prose strikes us as the remnant of an old Itihasa. In that chapter Janmejaya is admittedly the great-grandson of Arjuna and not an ancestor. It seems therefore certain that there was only one Janmejaya Parikshita and he was a descendant of the great heroes of the Mahabharata war. Granting, however, that there is a confusion about Janmejaya in the Mahabharata, how does it follow from this that the sin of Brahmahatya of which Janmejaya was absolved was the sin of the great war? It is indeed a long step to take from the mere mention of a Brahmahatya to the sin of waging a great war. The Shatapatha Brahmana gives no hint whatever as to what that Hatya was which Janmejaya had committed. In the chapter in the Shanti Parva, where this Vedic legend has been repeated, we find it stated that Janmejaya had killed a Brahmin by accident. Chapter II of the Adiparva, where the same Janmejaya Parikshita is mentioned, gives no clue whatever to the nature of his sin. In the great war, so far as it is described in the Mahabharata, only one Brahmin was killed, *viz.*, Drona. He was more a warrior than a Brahmin, and as he had come as a leader on the opposite side in order to kill others there was no sin whatever in killing him. The Dharma Shastra is clear on the point and has frequently been stated to be so in the Mahabharata itself. We fail to see how the simple mention of a Brahmahatya in the Shatapatha Brahmana can be expanded into and identified with the guilt of the Mahabharata war.

There is another passage in the Vedic Literature which has been made the basis of mistaken inferences. In the Brihadaranya Upanishad of the Shatapatha Brahmana Yajnavalkya is asked by his opponent in disputation, "Where were the Parikshitas" (sons of Parikshit)? Yajnavalkya answers, "Thither where all the Ashvamedha sacrificers go." This has led Weber to observe, "Consequently the Parikshitas must at that time have been altogether extinct. Yet their life and end must have been still fresh in the memory of the people and a subject of general curiosity" and again in another place,

"Janmejaya Parikshita appears in the last part of the Shatapatha Brahmana to be still fresh in the memory of the people with the rise and downfall of himself and his house." Now, so far as one can see, there is nothing in the passage of the Brihadaranya Upanishad above referred to which can suggest the idea that the sons of Parikshita fell or that their fall was terrible. Granting that the question and answer may be construed to convey the idea that there was a doubt in the questioner's mind about the sons of Parikshita having gone there, as perhaps he had their sin of Brahmahatya in his mind, how does it warrant the inference that the Parikshitas had any worldly fall? Is it believed that the Parikshitas were defeated in battle? On the contrary the inference subsequently made by Weber is that they were the leaders in the Mahabharata war and had secured a victory and not a fall by means of treachery and sin. To our mind the former inference of Weber is not only baseless but opposed to what he himself has propounded in the latter place. Moreover, the whole passage was not considered, for the answer went on to say "there where the performers of the horse-sacrifice go, *viz.*, beyond the world where there is a space as small as the wing of a fly or the edge of a razor, &c." The passage in question is only really meant to show, as can be seen from the commentary, that the performance of a horse-sacrifice led to the same goal where a sage could go by Adhyatma Vidya. Probably the questioner had not the sins of the Parikshitas at all in his mind even if they had committed any.

To take a resume, the absence of the mention of the Pandavas and the Mahabharata war in the Vedic Literature which does not purport to be a history of events cannot be taken to prove that the Pandavas never existed or that the war was never fought, nor can they, from the actions ascribed to them, be looked upon as imaginary heroes. Again, although Janmejaya Parikshita and his Brahmahatya are mentioned in the Shatapatha Brahmana there is nothing to show that that Brahmahatya was the guilt of the Mahabharata fight. Had it been so the Shatapatha Brahmana would very probably have said a word indicating the nature of the Brahmahatya. Nor does it seem that the Parikshitas had any worldly fall. On the contrary they were remembered for their great horse-sacrifices, the performance of which shows that they were in the height of their glory.

Having so far shown that the Pandavas were real beings and that they and not Janmejaya were the parties to the great war, we will proceed to give a sketch of the events described in the Mahabharata omitting mythological stories or simplifying them where possible.

CHAPTER III.

THE ANCESTORS OF THE PANDAVAS.

OF the lunar race of Kshatriyas, supposed to have been born of the moon from Ila, the daughter of Manu, Pururava was the first king of note. The loves of Pururava and Urvashi, a celestial nymph, are mentioned in the Rig Veda and have been immortalised by Kalidasa in his well-known drama Vikramorvashiyam. The next king of importance in the line was Yayati. The story of Yayati and his two queens, Devayani and Sharmishtha, is one of the most interesting episodes given in the Mahabharata and deserves to be given here in detail. The Kshatriyas of the lunar race appear to have been still beyond the Indus, for Yayati's kingdom is said to have been contiguous with the kingdom of Vrishaparva, the king of Asuras, who have been most properly identified with the Aryans of Iran. Sharmishtha was the daughter of the king of Iran, and Devayani was the daughter of his preceptor Shukra. The two girls once went out on a forest excursion and while bathing in a well fell out in consequence of an accidental interchange of clothes. The imperious Brahmin girl abused the daughter of her master as if she were a slave, whereon Sharmishtha in the heat of anger pushed her into the well. Yayati came there by chance and being attracted by the cries of Devayani saved her life by helping her out of the well. She offered herself in reward for his gallant act and Yayati married Devayani with the consent of her father. She had yet to take revenge on her friend and insisted that Sharmishtha should be bestowed upon her as a slave. Vrishaparva had no recourse but to accept this humiliating demand of Devayani and handed over his guilty daughter to the married couple as their slave.

Devayani confined her rival for years in the palace of Yayati, but little did she dream that the vengeance she had taken was in reality a boon conferred on Sharmishtha. One day she was rudely awakened from her dream by the sight of two handsome young boys curiously resembling her husband in appearance and she learnt on inquiry that they were the sons of Yayati himself by her rival. In her rage she flew to her father for vengeance upon her own husband and Shukra cursed him by declaring that he would be prematurely old. The senseless Devayani thus harmed herself in seeking to harm her rival and in the end had to implore her father to assuage his curse. Shukra added that the old age was transferable. Yayati now asked his sons one by one to take his infirmity, but every one of them declined to do so with the exception of Puru. For years Yayati enjoyed the pleasures of this world with the youth borrowed from Puru. At last he exclaimed, so the poet says:

> Desire stops not by gain of things desired,
> But fiercer burns like fire by oblations fed.
> All the gold, grain and women of this world,
> Would not suffice one man; be content.

Yayati called his son Puru and transferring to him his youth took upon himself the age he had lent him and taking his two queens with him retired to the forest like all the great kings of ancient India. He blessed Puru for his filial act and told him that sovereignty would continue in his line.

The story of Yayati is not only beautiful for its moral: but is also historically important. We have already seen that the lunar Aryans were still beyond the Indus. Again the intermixture of the two castes, Brahmins and Kshatriyas, was then a common thing. Thirdly, Yayati had five sons by name Yadu, Turvasu, Druhyu, Puru and Anu, the last two by Sharmishtha. From Yadu sprang the Yadavas, from Turvasu the Yavanas, from Druhyu the Bhojas, from Puru the Paurvas, latterly known as the Bharatas, and from Anu the Mlenchha peoples. Yayati is thus represented as the progenitor of many clans, three of which, the Yadavas, the Bhojas and the Pauravas, entered India, while the fourth, the Yavanas, went towards the west. It is possible that there is an interchange of names in this enumeration and the Yavanas should perhaps have been represented as the descendants of Anu which corresponds most in sound with Ion while the Mlenchha people should have been spoken of as the descendants of Turvasu, a name which sounds like the Turan of the Persians and the Turks of modern history. The mythological story of the transference of old age may be thus simplified historically. Yayati probably, though advanced in age, did not share the royal power with his grown up sons by Devayani, who may be believed to have inherited her rashness. They wanted him to resign that power and finding the old man still in vigour and still obstinate rebelled against him. They were thus expelled by Yayati, who was supported in this action by his son Puru. Eventually Puru succeeded to the chiefship of the clan by his filial conduct.

The first king of note among the descendants of Puru is Dushyanta. The story of Dushyanta and Shakuntala the Apsara is known to every reader of Sanskrit poetry, for the beautiful drama of Kalidas 'the lost ring,' about which Goethe is so enthusiastic in his admiration, is based on that history. But the Shakuntala of the Mahabharata is vastly different from the Shakuntala of Kalidas. She is not a refined timorous lady as Kalidas has made her, but an honest country girl full of the dignity of moral greatness. She had married the king by choice when he had come accidently to her father's hermitage during her father's absence in the jungles, and there was no witness to their marriage. And when, after some years, she went with her son from her parents' hut to the capital of her husband, and the king in open court denied having ever married her, she exclaimed, "Truth is more precious than kings and even children," and she disclaimed to seek the company any longer of a man who had no respect for truth, even though he was her husband. At last the king, who had only sought this device to convince his people, took her into his household on hearing a voice from heaven that she was indeed his wife. Bharata was the offspring of this union of choice and moral strength, and became the most illustrious king of the family of Puru. He appears to have conquered and sacrificed in India as far down as the confluence of the Jamna and the Ganges, and the Shatapatha Brahman quotes a historical verse in Kanda XIX eulogising him for the horse sacrifices he performed on the banks of the Ganges and the Jamna. He gave his name not only to his descendants but also to the whole country, for India down to the present day is known in the Sanskrit Literature as the land of Bharata.

The descendants of Bharata were a powerful people, who inhabited the Punjab and gradually extended their settlements southwards towards the Ganges and the Jamna. The Bharatas are spoken of even in the Vedic Literature as a brave people (Dutt's India). One of the descendants of Bharata, by name Hasti, founded Hastinapura on the western bank of the Ganges, and it became the capital of a new country, for it appears that the Bharatas now permanently moved from the Punjab towards the Ganges and Hasti's great-grandson Kuru gave his name to the fertile tract between the upper courses of the Ganges and the Jamna and also to the west of the latter river, northwards of Dehli. The Kurus now became a flourishing people and they are frequently spoken of along with the Panchalas (who had settled to the east of the Ganges and a little southward) in the Brahmanas as a highly civilized and gifted people.

The kings of the Kurus, who subsequently reigned in this fertile and happy land, have been mentioned in the previous chapter. Here we may take up the line from Shantanu. Shantanu had a son Bhishma (by the river Ganges [1]), who is one of the most beautiful characters in the Mahabharata war. After Ganga had deserted Shantanu he fell in love with a fisher girl, by name Satyavati, but she refused to marry him unless the king promised her that her son would be his heir. Shantanu would not disinherit Bhishma who, however, of his own accord relieved his father from difficulty, and not

[1] *See* note IV.

only renounced his right to the heirship but resolved not to marry at all so that there might be no progeny from him to quarrel with Satyavati and the sons that might be born to her. This resolve he carried to his grave, and his great self-denial and his pious character have hallowed his name, which is always mentioned with high reverence by the Aryans of India.

Shantanu had two sons by Satyavati, one of whom died in infancy. Vichitravirya succeeded his father in the kingship of the Kurus, but he died childless, though Bhishma had married him to two wives, Ambika and Ambalaya, whom he had brought by force from the king of Kashi. Satyawati had, before her marriage with Shantanu, a son born to her by the sage Parashara. That son was none other than Vyasa, the author of the Mahabharata and the compiler of the Vedas. Vyasa was now called to raise progeny on the widows of his half-brother by Satyawati with the consent of Bhishma, the guardian of the family, and two sons, Dhritarashtra and Pandu, were thus born to Vichitravirya by Niyoga or levirate as it was called among the Jews. A third son Vidura was born to Vyasa by a "Dasi." Dhritarashtra was blind, and Pandu ruled the kingdom for some time, when he retired to and died in a forest. Dhritarashtra, it is said, had by his wife Gandhari (daughter of the king of Gandhara) a hundred sons, the chief of whom were Duryodhana and Duhshasana. It is these that fought the great battle, called the Mahabharata war, with the Pandavas or the sons of Pandu. How these sons were born to Pandu we shall describe in the next chapter.

CHAPTER IV.

THEIR BIRTH, EARLY LIFE AND MARRIAGE WITH DRAUPADI.

THE Mahabharata relates that Pandu took to hunting, leaving the kingdom to be governed by Dhritarashtra under the guidance of Bhishma. He loved to live in the forest with his two wives, and roamed about killing deer and other beasts of the jungle. One day he killed a deer in the act of copulating with his mate, and was stunned to see that he had in fact killed a Rishi, who had in his fancy assumed that animal form. The Rishi cursed him that he too would diein the same condition. Pandu, touched by remorse thereafter, gave up associating with his wives and went to the Himalayas with the object of performing austerities. For years he lived a life of penance, but remembering that no man could have absolution unless he had sons asked his wives Kunti and Madri to resort to Niyoga for that purpose. Kunti had obtained from a Rishi in her maidenhood five Mantras by which she could call up five deities. These she now called and had by Dharma (Righteousness), Vayu (Wind), Indra (God of War), three sons born to her, who were named Dharma, Bhima and Arjuna, respectively. She gave the remaining two Mantras to Madri, her co-wife, and she too had two sons by the Ashwini Kumar (Twin Gods of Beauty), who were named Nakul and

Sahadeo. Pandu was now satisfied, but forgetting his curse one day fell a victim to his amorous inclination. Madri burned herself upon his pyre, while Kunti with her five sons was reached by the Brahmans of the forest to Hastinapura. The sons of Dhritarashtra, jealous of these new members, raised some objections, but Dhritarashtra and Bhishma hailed them as the sons of Pandu and admitted them to the family.

Such is the mythological account of the birth of the Pandavas, the heroes of the Mahabharata war. All nations and all religions have invested the origin of their heroes and their prophets with mysterious and supernatural surroundings. And we need not wonder how the Hindus attribute divine origin to their heroes supposed to have been born five thousand years ago. There are, however, some who look to noble and divine deeds only and care little for divine or supernatural birth. Such men like to simplify mythological stories into their natural aspects, and one would not find it difficult to rationalise the above account if one omits the curse and the divine Mantras mentioned therein.

We may here state who Kunti and Madri were. Kunti, the Mahabharata relates, was the daughter of Shura, the father of Vasudeva, and grandfather of Krishna. She was called Pritha, or the big, and was given in adoption to the king of Kunti Bhoja, who was his (Shura's) paternal uncle's son, and was hence called Kunti. She married Pandu at a Swayamvara. The Bhoja kingdom was towards the south of Hastinapura and extended probably over the western limits of Central India. The Bhojas and the Yadavas, as we have already seen, were kindred races. Madri was the daughter of the king of the Madras whose country lay towards the frontier. The Madras were presumably a very fair people, coming, as they did, from a colder climate. It seems it was a fashion for Aryan kings of India to marry a daughter of that country. Bhishma got Madri for Pandu by giving presents to the Madra king. Madri's brother, Shalya, was a leader in the Mahabharata war and fought against the Pandavas.

It appears probable that Pandu, after he had established himself firmly on the throne of the Kurus, gave himself up to the pleasures of hunting and to the company of his wives, and lived mostly in the cool regions of the Himalayas. It is not difficult also to believe that he soon fell a prey to the pursuit of pleaure. Either during his life-time or after his death his wives raised by Niyoga five sons, for progeny was valued beyond everything among the ancient Aryans of India, especially among kings, a fact we see even in these days. As might have been expected the sons of Pritha were strong, while those of Madri were handsome. All of them were fine warriors and lived a noble life; and noble and divine deeds, such was the belief of the ancient Aryans, betokened noble parentage. A story in the Chhando-yoga Upanishad clearly brings this firm belief of the ancient Aryans. When Satyakama Jabala went to a sage for Upadesha or teaching and was asked his name and his father's name, he said "I am Satyakama Jabala and my mother said to me she did not know who my father was." "Thou art the son of a Brahman," said the sage, "for thou speakest the truth." We not therefore wonder that the Pandavas were attributed a divine origin by their contemporaries and their successors.

Sceptics and questioners are, however, found in every age and the Mahabharata itself furnishes the evidence that the legitimacy of the Pandavas was doubted even then. Some said in Hastinapura that they were the sons of Pandu, and others said, how could they be, for Pandu was dead long since. But after all they said "welcome are they; happy are we to hail the sons of Pandu." [1] It was this doubt probably about their origin which was at the root of the ever-increasing jealousy which sprung between them and the sons of Dhritarashtra and which at last ended in the great conflict on the plains of Kuru Kshetra.

Yudhishthira or Dharma was older than Duryodhana by one year, while Bhima and Duryodhana are said in the Mahabharata to have been born on the same day. The other brothers appear therefore to have been younger each at least by one year. It is not mentioned how old the Pandavas were when they were brought to Hastinapura, but their early training was imparted to them in the ancestral home under the eye of Drona, a Brahmin teacher versed in the Vedas as well as in archery. He was specially engaged for the purpose and taught the hundred and six boys given to him as pupils with the same care. But Arjuna, the middle Pandava, was his favourite pupil and outshone all the others in the art of throwing the arrow. The bow and the arrow

[1] Ahuh kechinnatasyaite tasyaite iti chapare, &c. 17 and 18, Adhyayas Adiparva.

was the highest weapon in those days as the gun and the bullet is in these, and we shall have to speak of this weapon at greater length in a subsequent chapter. Bhima and Duryodhana were athletes and became equally versed in wrestling and the use of the mace, but Bhima was the stronger of the two. The superior strength and skill of the Pandavas added fuel to the fire of hatred already burning fiercely in the heart of Duryodhana and his brothers, and they one day threw Bhima while asleep into the Ganges on the banks of which they had all gone to play. When Bhima did not return with the rest of his brothers, his mother Kunti was in great wail. Bhima is said to have been taken to the Nagaloka by serpents and there to have drunk the nectar of life. He returned safe next day to the surprise of his enemies and the joy of the Pandavas and their mother. Probably Bhima did not die in the cold water in consequence of a snake-bite and came up alive the better and stronger for the venom which he had digested.

The education of the princes was finished in a few years and the result was exhibited in a tournament which has been beautifully described in the Mahabharata and which shows the manner of education imparted in Aryan India to the sons of kings. A large arena or amphitheatre was erected outside the city by orders of Dhritarashtra at the instance and under the auspices of Drona. On an appointed day the inhabitants of the city flocked to the theatre to witness the grand tournament. Blind Dhritarashtra with his wife Gandhari, Kunti and other members of the royal family went and had their seats in the appointed places. Now sounded the trumpets announcing the coming of the exhibitors when the crowd became quiet, and Drona, who looked grave with his white beard and white dress, led the princes one by one into the arena. There they exhibited their skill in bending the bow and throwing the javelin, riding the horse and driving the elephant, fighting with the scimitar or wielding the mace. The audience shouted cries of acclamation when Duryodhana and Bhima, of splendid physique, entered the lists with maces in their hands, and as they moved about the field and struck each other at every opportunity with force, there was a division among the spectators, some betting for Duryodhana and others for Bhima. Drona finding the division and fight assuming an unpleasant aspect asked his son Ashwatthama to stop the fighting and announced that he would now bring forth his best and most favourite pupil, dearer to him, as he said, than his own son. Then entered Arjuna, clothed in a golden armour with protection covers for his hands and his head, with the bow in his left hand and the arrow in his right. Trumpets blew, conches were filled and Dhritarashtra inquired what the matter was, when Vidura told him that Arjuna, the best of archers, had entered the field. Arjuna now showed his skill at the bow, sending five arrows in quick succession, as if they were one, through the mouth of a swinging boar made of iron, and performing similar other feats, and then showed his mastery over Astras or supernatural missiles (of which we shall speak in a subsequent chapter). He then moved about in a chariot ascending and descending from it with ease and agility and practised with the mace and the sword. Acclamations after acclamations greeted him at every act and trumpets blew again when he had finished. Scarcely had their sound ceased when an uproar rose at the entrance, and a warrior, tall and strong, striking his arms, making a sound, deep and sonorous with a *slap*, bearing the bow and arrow, entered the lists. Drona and his pupils and every man and woman in the amphitheatre looked towards the entrance, and Karna bowing to Drona and Kripa almost slightingly said to Arjuna, "Whatever feat thou hast performed I will. Think not high of thyself." The spectators sprung to their feet in amazement and curiosity, and while Duryodhana's face brightened with delight, Arjuna felt a little abashed and enraged. Drona, however, permitted Karna to proceed, and he exhibited his skill at the bow, performing one by one all the feats shown by Arjuna. "Welcome thee, Oh warrior," said Duryodhana embracing him, "Be my friend and enjoy the kingdom of the Kurus." "I value nothing more than thy friendship," said Karna, "I earnestly long for a duel with Arjuna." "Well spoken," said Duryodhana, "thou art indeed well-fitted to place thy foot on the neck of my enemies." Arjuna naturally thought he had been insulted, and cried "Oh Karna, I will instantly send thee to that fate which awaits those who come in uncalled and speak unasked." "But," retorted Karna, "the arena is a public place and prowess is the passport for every act. I can punish thee even in the presence of thy Acharya." Drona now permitted Arjuna to fight a duel with Karna, and Arjuna embracing his brothers and bowing to his preceptor stood ready for the fight. Karna also embraced his new friend and prepared to receive him; the audience was now divided between the two warriors, but Kunti swooned, for she knew not what to do. At this point to her relief stepped forth Kripa well versed in the laws of duels, and cried "Here is Arjuna, son of Kunti and of Pandu, of the race of the Kurus; proclaim thou thy name, for kings' sons fight not a duel with men of unknown family." At these words down went Karna's head like a wet lotus hanging down under a drizzling rain. "Acharya," interposed Duryodhana, "there are three classes of kings—those who are so by birth, those who are brave, and those who command armies. But if Arjuna has an objection to fight with one who is not an actual king, I bestow on Karna the kingdom of the Angas." Immediately a white umbrella was held over his head and they saluted him with the words "success to thee." "What shall I give thee in return," said the grateful Karna. "Nothing but thy friendship" replied Duryodhana. Here entered an old man, a charioteer by caste, supporting himself on a stick and shedding tears of joy at the fortune and fame to which his son had suddenly attained. Karna in respect bowed down his head which the old man wetted with tears in bestowing on him the kiss of blessing. At this Bhima laughed loudly and cried "Oh Karna, thou dost not deserve to be killed by Arjuna. Throw away the bow and take up a whip. Thou dost not deserve even the kingdom of the Angas." Karna throbbing with rage only looked at the sun in the heaven, but Duryodhana shot forth from among his brothers and said "Bhimasena, you speak unfairly. Strength is the highest merit of a Kshatriya and the lowest Kshatriya if strong may fight. Even Brahmans are born of Kshatriyas, for Vishwamitra and others became Brahmins by their worth. Everybody knows how you were born. This warrior deserves to be the king of the whole world, what then of the Angas alone? He who does not approve of my action let him step forward and bend the bow." Consternation reigned in the whole arena at these words, but the sun at that time set, and Duryodhana taking Karna by the hand walked out of the arena followed by his brothers by the light of torches.

We have thought fit to give the above passage *in extenso* not only as an instance of the many splendid spirited dialogues which are the peculiar charm of the Mahabharata but because it so finely brings out the manners of the times and the characters of the actors. We feel as if we are transplanted into the midst of those Western Aryans of old whose chivalry has been beautifully described by Scot. We feel we are in the company of stern warriors, bold, fearless and truthful, of men who fought duels under strict rules of honour, of men who honoured merit as high as parentage, of women who lived an exemplary life though they had by a regrettable chance once gone astray in early life. The characters strike us as real but not prosaic, and are brought out in bold relief: the proud Duryodhana, the vain yet faithful Karna, the impetuous Bhima, and the strong but steady Arjuna, and we cannot but admit that each in his own way is an exemplary yet inimitable man.

The tournament over and it may almost be called the embryo of the future conflict, Dhritarashtra went home ruminating over the split which had evidently sprung between the cousins. He fell an easy prey to the advice of a minister (Kanika by name) the principles of whose machiavelian policy are well set forth in the Mahabharata and are known as Kanika Niti. He lent a willing ear to a plot which his sons now concocted to destroy the Pandavas by underhand means. A palace with walls filled with lac and other combustible materials was erected in Varanavata, a distant town, and the five brothers with their mother were asked to go there to reside for a time in order to prevent a quarrel between the brothers. Vidura, however, came to know the danger and warned Yudhishthira of it, speaking to him at the time of departure in a Mlenchha or un-Aryan tongue. Diggers sent by him had already prepared a subterranean passage from within the house to a distance from the town; and the five brothers and their mother escaped by it when the palace was burnt as if by accident on the next day of their arrival, though people believed that they were all burnt within.

We need not pursue the warriors in their wanderings in the forest. It may be that Bhima married Hidimba, the daughter of a Rakshasa or cannibal, but the story of Baka is evidently a childish interpolation of later times. The brothers dressed as Brahmins emerged out of their obscurity at the Swayamvara of Draupadi which was shortly held at the capital of the Panchalas.

The Panchala kingdom as described in the Mahabharata may be supposed to have extended from Rohilkhand in the north to the Chambal in the south. The portion of it to the north of the Ganges of which Ahichhatra was the capital had been wrested from Drupada, the king of the Panchalas, by the Kurus led by Drona and his 106 pupils. Drupada now ruled to the south in Kampilya and was burning to have his vengeance on Drona. He is said to have performed a sacrifice from which sprang Krishnā or Draupadi, the future queen of the Pandavas, and a son named Dhrishtadyumna, who was destined to kill Drona. Drupada wished to secure Arjuna for his son-in-law, but not knowing his whereabouts proclaimed a Swayamvara of his beautiful daughter at which the victor was to bend a bow specially constructed for the occasion and shoot arrows specially made at a moving target hanging in the sky. Kings and princes assembled at the capital of the southern Panchalas and were received and encamped to the north of the town in a great camp, having streets laid with sandal-scented water and beautified with arches at the gate. On the appointed day the competitors assembled in the Swayamvara hall and seated themselves on golden seats spread over with costly coverings, anxious to have a look at the beauteous bride. Krishnā having bathed and put on a superb dress and precious ornaments now entered the hall bearing in the hand a gold-laced garland. The preceptor of the family of the Panchalas sacrificed at the family altar and taking the blessing of the Brahmanas stopped all music. Dhrishtadyumna now took his sister by the hand and addressed the assembly of princes and Brahmanas in a clear and sonorous voice: "Here is this bow," said he, "and here the arrows. Whoever will send them in the hole of the target hanging above, him shall my sister marry." The kings and princes assembled, smitten with love and jealous of each other, one by one tried their hand at the bow but could not even string it. Abashed and enraged they returned to their seats. Karna then stepped forth, took up the bow, strung it and was about to take up the arrows when Draupadi exclaimed "I am not prepared to marry a charioteer." His face fell and the bow fell from his hands and looking up at the sun he too returned to his seat. There was now a pause and Arjuna rose from among the Brahmans. There was a murmur both of approbation and disapprobation among them as he went towards the bow. But heeding not either, he took up the bow and having strung it sent the arrows in quick succession through the hole of the target. A cry of applause from the Brahmins hailed him. They said, "A Brahmin has risen superior on the field. A Brahmin has won Draupadi." Yudhishthira with his brothers now stood up and without waiting any further started back for his home. Arjuna taking hold of the hand of Draupadi, whose face was radiant with the smile of love and whose heart was filled with delight at having secured a husband valiant as the lion, followed her.

Such is the description of the Swayamvara of Draupadi and it speaks volumes of the manners of the times. It shows how Kshatriyas and Brahmins vied with each other even in the field of arms, how Brahmins often won and married Kshatriya daughters, how brides were grown up and fearless at the time of marriage, how princesses followed their husbands gladly into obscurity and privation. When the brothers reached home, they said to their mother that they had brought alms and she asked them to share them among themselves. This is the fantastic explanation given in the Mahabharata of the marriage of the five brothers with a single woman. Nobody would believe that a casual command given by mistake would be obeyed so literally, nor is it likely that Kunti would have said what she is made to say. Alms, ordinarily, would be grain, and grain had to be cooked before it could be partaken by the brothers. Other explanations have also been given in the Mahabharata, but are equally unsatisfying. A sentence, however, has been preserved in the epic, a fossil as we have said elsewhere, which gives a clue to the right solution of the question. "This is our family custom," said Yudhishthira to the wavering king of the Panchalas, "and we do not feel we are transgressing Dharma in following it." We shall have to return to this subject in another place.

CHAPTER V.

THE FOUNDING OF INDRAPRASTHA OR DEHLI AND ITS FIRST IMPERIAL ASSEMBLAGE.

SHRIKRISHNA first appears on the scene in the Mahabharata here and he is introduced without any reference to his previous history (nor has his history been separately given in any place in the Epic). He was one of those princes who had come to witness the grand Swayamvara and was glad to find that his cousins were not only alive but had also won the beauteous bride. He paid his respects to Kunti, his paternal aunt, congratulated the Pandavas on their success and made valuable presents to them on the occasion of their marriage. Dhritarashtra trembled in his shoes when he heard that the sons of Kunti were alive and were married to the daughter of the powerful Panchala king. The crafty old monarch now protested his great love for the sons of Pandu as dear to him, he said, as his own sons and sent Vidura with many presents to call them back to Hastinapura. The Pandavas were quite happy to return home and went there accompanied by Krishna. They were received by Bhishma and others with great affection and honour. Dhritarashtra now divided the kingdom between his sons and the Pandavas in order to avoid future dissensions between them, assigning the latter as their portion

Khandavaprastha and the territory to the west of the Jamna, a very large part of which was covered with thick jungle of which the brave warriors, so the old monarch said, would not be afraid.

The brothers founded a new capital in their kingdom which they called Indraprastha, of which the remnants are even now pointed out by the side of the modern Dehli. The capital was soon filled with Brahmanas from all quarters, traders who spoke different languages, artificers of every description. Slowly the capital was also surrounded by gardens filled with mango trees and pleasure houses. The country had to be cleared of its forests and the Nagas, who are unquestionably a mythological transformation of the aboriginal people who molested the Aryans in their peaceful settlements. An atrocious device was adopted which has also been transformed into the legend of the burning of the Khandava forest. Agni or fire, it is stated, once appeared before Arjuna and Krishna and requested the two warriors to assist him in devouring the forest which was under the special protection of Indra or the God of rain. Agni gave a divine bow called Gandiva to Arjuna and he and Krishna watched while Agni devoured the forest. Not a single animal was allowed to escape and the fierce fire raged for fifteen days reducing the vast jungle to ashes and destroying thousands of beasts and birds and probably human beings. Only six are represented to have escaped, *viz.*, Takshaka Ashvasena (of whom we shall speak again towards the end), Maya and four sparrows whose miraculous preservation it would be out of place to give here. This device of burning a large forest and of destroying the beasts, and probably the jungly aborigines transformed latterly into Nagas and Asuras, who interfered with the cultivation of land, does indeed seem atrocious and would not be tolerated in these days. It was, however, in those days of first settlement believed to be a sacrifice to Agni and was not looked upon as heinous, and the country thus cleared of forest and the molesters of peaceful agriculture soon attained to a prosperous condition under the strong but just rule of the five brothers.

The union of the Pandavas and the Yadavas was now further cemented by the marriage of Arjuna to Subhadra, sister of Shrikrishna. It was not a marriage of reciprocal love as is represented by modern poets. According to the Mahabharata it was a marriage by seizure, for it is stated that Arjuna while on a pilgrimage to Dwarka saw the beautiful girl in a festival wherein men and women had gone out from Dwarka to the Raivataka hill. By the advice of Krishna, who said he did not know whether Subhadra liked him or not, Arjuna forcibly seized and carried her away in his chariot. Krishna's brother Balarama was about to pursue and chastise the abductor, but was prevailed upon by Krishna to acquiesce in the marriage. Of this union was born Abhimanyu, the favourite son of Arjuna and nephew of Krishna. Draupadi too had five sons born to her from the five Pandavas.

Conscious of their increased strength and emboldened by their alliance with the Yadavas and the Panchalas, the Pandavas now began to revolve schemes for the assumption of universal sovereignty, and Yudhishthira called and consulted Krishna as to how far the scheme was practicable. The idea of a Chakravarti or Emperor of India originated, according to Krishna's explanation, in the humiliation of the Kshatriya race by the Brahman Parashurama. The Kshatriyas who escaped death in the war of extermination waged by that relentless Brahman warrior against them, formed themselves into a coalition of which one was appointed the Chakravarti or the Emperor. What was, however, intended originally to oppose the Brahmins became in the end the cause of their own destruction, for every ambitious king aspired to be the Chakravarti and tried to subject others to his rule. Jarasandha, Krishna said, was the Emperor then and had kept hundreds of princes in confinement at his capital Rajagriha, subsequently known as Patali Putra or modern Patna. Even Krishna had fled from Mathura and gone to Dwarka in fear of him. But as Hansa and Dhimbhaka, two warriors whom he had in his service, were dead, it was easy for Bhima supported by Krishna and Arjuna to slay him in single combat. Permitted by Yudhishthira forth started the three warriors in the garb of Brahmin mendicants. Reaching the city of Rajagriha by forced marches they entered it by a side way and struck and broke the great drum that was kept on the gate. Walking through the streets they took garlands from a flowerman by force and bedecking themselves with them defiantly entered the palace of Jarasandha, no one stopping them either through fear or in respect for their dress. Jarasandha received them in due form offering them water and honey, but as none of them accepted the presents his suspicions were roused and he asked them the reason of their strange actions and false garb. Krishna replied "know thou that we are thy enemies and therefore have entered the city by a side way. We are decked in flowers because victory greets those who put on flowers. We are Kshatriyas ready to fight with thee. Come, fight with any of us if thou art not prepared to release the princes whom thou hast unjustly confined." Jarasandha now knew the truth and accepted the challenge and prepared to fight with Bhima without arms. It was a fight for victory or death, and having taken the blessings of the Brahmans and taking off his crown he stepped into the list. There the two gladiators with their arms only as their weapons fought untired, unceasing, taking no food nor rest till at last on the 14th day Jarasandha retired seeking rest for a time. Krishna beckoned to Bhima not to lose the opportunity, and Bhima springing upon his tired foe whirled him round, broke his back-bone by the pressure of his knee, and taking hold of his legs tore the body into two halves. It was a terrible scene, and the roar of the dying man and triumphant warrior sent a thrill of terror through the whole palace. The three then threw the dead body at the gate of the palace and left the place in Jarasandha's chariot.

Such is the awful description of the mortal fight between Jarasandha and Bhima. There may be a great deal of exaggeration in it, but we cannot doubt the vein of reality which runs through the whole narration. That the art of building up a strong body had reached great success in ancient India, we may fairly accept from what we see of athletes even now in this country and prize fights ending in the death of one of the combatants were formerly witnessed even in western countries The fight between Jarasandha and Bhima, as described in the Mahabharata, is not so absurd as it has subsequently been made by later poets, who state that the two halves of Jarasandha's body joined together as often as they were severed, and Krishna at last asked Bhima to change sides in throwing the halves which then could not join to form a body

Jarasandha destroyed, there remained nobody who could oppose the Pandavas in their ambitious designs To assume, however, universal sovereignty a formal conquest of the four quarters of the known world was necessary, and Arjuna, Bhima, Nakula and Sahadeva, taking divisions of armies with them, went north, east, west and south, receiving submission from and fighting with, where necessary, the various peoples who lived in those regions An enumeration of these people is made in the Mahabharata and is very important as it shows the geographical knowledge at the time of Chandra Gupta if not of the Pandavas themselves Having thus conquered the whole world the Pandavas with the advice of Krishna decided to declare themselves the master of the Aryan world Among the ancient Aryans of India every event was celebrated by the performance of a sacrifice as in modern Europe by the delivery of a speech The assumption of universal sovereignty was in ancient India signalised by the performance of what was called the Rajasuyayajnya A great hall like the amphi-theatre which was just erected in Dehli had been built by the Asura Maya in gratitude for his deliverance from the Khandava conflagration. It was built of costly materials, brought from the Himalayas, and the architect had employed his skill so successfully that in some places hard ground looked like a watery surface and water looked like hard ground. Hundreds of princes assembled from the four quarters to pay homage to the Emperor and were put up in beautiful palaces specially built outside the town. Brahmans were feasted from day to day and the sacrificial fire burned with the oblations of the flesh of various animals. Bhishma and Drona, Duryodhana and his brothers were also present and were assigned honorary duties in connection with the Imperial sacrifice. Duryodhana was especially charged with the duty of receiving presents from the assembled kings.

On the last day of the sacrifice on which every one present had the opportunity of bathing with holy waters (Avabhritasnana) with the Emperor, Brahmans and princes assembled in the inner sacrificial grounds, Bhishma according to custom called upon Yudhishthira to make Argha or presents to the assembled kings. The Emperor asked Bhishma who deserved the first honour. Whereon Bhishma declared that Krishna was the proper person to begin with. Sahadeva then at the command of the Emperor presented Krishna with Argha, which he accepted according to the rules of the ceremony. The first place of honour is always a cause of contention and Shishupala, the king of the Chedis, rose up in protest. He upbraided Bhishma for his wrong advice and attributed it to his old age. He then reviled Krishna himself for his acquiescence in accepting the first place when there were present older men than himself like his father Vasudeva and Drupada, wiser men like Vyasa and Drona, and mightier kings like Duryodhana and Shalya. Bhishma calmly explained that Krishna rightly deserved the first place as he was the mightiest, the wisest and the most honoured of all. He was in fact the incarnation of Vishnu. This gave a fresh subject for reviling to Shishupala who was not one of those who believed so. He came down upon Krishna for deluding the world by false pretentions to divinity and upbraided Bhishma as a supporter of false claims who deserved to be stoned to death or burned like the old bird in the well-known fable by his brother princes. This was too much even for the old philosophic Bhishma and he exclaimed in the heat of passion "My death is at my will, I count the kings present, not so much as a straw. It is useless to argue without end. Here is Krishna who deserves to be honoured first and has been so honoured by us. Let him who disapproves of this come forward and fight with him." Shishupala stepped forth at once and challenged Shrikrishna to fight. Krishna said: "I have pardoned thee one hundred times according to my promise but cannot pardon thee any longer." With these words he cut his head off by throwing his discus. It was a ghastly end to a joyous beginning. The princes assembled were cowed down and raised no protest. But there were many who burned within with a desire to wreak vengeance on the party guilty of open assassination. The sacrifice, however, was quietly finished and

Yudhishthira dismissed the princes to their homes with costly and suitable presents.

The assembling of princes for the purpose of proclaiming the assumption of the Imperial Power cannot always be a successful proceeding. Moreover the display of wealth and power rouses jealousy in the heart of the evil-disposed, while the coming together of many persons whose high position makes them sensitive on points of honour, unavoidably furnishes occasion to many for being displeased and discontented. Thus in spite of his efforts in the right direction, Yudhishthira soon found that he had by his actions given a point to the height of glory to which he had risen and that there must be a descent for some time at least, however much he might fondly hope that there were pinnacles after pinnacles of glory rising one above the other like the peaks of the Himalayas. He had created an unconquerable feeling of hatred and envy in the heart of his cousin which soon bore its evil fruit as we shall see in the next chapter.

CHAPTER VI.

THE DISGRACEFUL GAME AT DICE AND ITS CONSEQUENCES.

DURYODHANA returned home burning with the desire to humble the Pandavas and to possess himself of their wealth and called to counsel his friends Karna and Shakuni. Open attack was impossible, and Shakuni suggested that they should take advantage of Yudhishthira's failing, *viz.*, his love for the dice. The ancient Aryans of India were as fond of gambling as their brethren of Germany, and the rules of honour did not allow a challenge given to be declined. The trio decided upon making false dice and inviting Yudhishthira to a game with Shakuni, who was an expert, and to cheat him out of his kingdom and wealth. Old Dhritarashtra was prevailed upon to consent to the plot by his ambitious son who gave most glorious descriptions of Yudhishthira's wealth, swelled as it had been by the presents he had received from the kings of India. He directed the erection of an assembly-room in imitation of the wonderful hall built for Yudhishthira by Maya and sent Vidura, in spite of his warnings, to invite Yudhishthira on pretext of seeing the great hall built by Duryodhana. Vidura went to Indraprastha and delivered the message to king Yudhishthira, and added of his own accord: "You may do what you think best, for gambling is a dangerous thing." With a heavy heart, and saying that the inevitable must happen, the king started with his brothers and his beautiful queen and reached Hastinapura in due time. There they were joyously received by their friends and relations, and the next day the five brothers went to the new hall where many princes and respectable men had assembled to greet them. "Let us have a game at dice," said Shakuni. "Gambling," replied Yudhishthira, "is a sin and a kind of fraud. Do not conquer me in this disreputable fashion. Aryas do not speak un-Aryan language nor walk in the paths of fraud." "A strong man," rejoined Shakuni, "conquers a weak one, a learned man a fool, but nobody looks upon that as a fraud. Why should a man clever at dice not conquer one who is less so? But if you think it is fraud you are at liberty to decline." It was too much for Yudhishthira, and saying that it was not his wont to refuse when called upon to play, he started the game without more ado. Stake after stake he lost, and maddened by his continuous failure he staked successively his wealth, his kingdom, his sons, his brothers and at last himself. "There still remains your wife," said Shakuni, with the sting of a gambler. "Have one more stake and you may win back everything." "I stake my wife," said the senseless king, "the beautiful Draupadi, neither short nor tall, neither thin nor bulky, with eyes as large and white and with breath as fragrant as an autumnal lotus flower; she who is as beautiful as kind and as well-behaved as a man may ever wish his wife to be. Her I stake. Shakuni, play." "Shame, shame," cried the spectators, who could not bear to see the disgraceful game; but nothing abashed Shakuni played and cried, "I have won, I have won." The joy of the trio knew no bounds, and Duryodhana called upon Vidura to go and bring Draupadi to the hall that she may be sent as a slave and made to work in the household and sweep the ground. "Fool," cried the outspoken Vidura, "thou art doomed; speak not unspeakable things; do not exasperate the lions; seest not thou that thou art overhanging a precipice?" The infatuated monarch however heeded him not and said to his servant Pratikami, "Go thou to Draupadi, tell her that she has been vanquished at game, and bring her here." The man went to Draupadi and spoke to her as desired, and returning, asked in the name of the clever queen of the Pandavas whether a man who had already staked himself away had a right to stake his wife. "Fool, thou art afraid of the Pandavas," said Duryodhana who was not to be balked by such nice subtleties, and he asked his brother Duhshasana to go and bring Draupadi to the assembly-hall. Off started Duhshasana, and entering the apartment of the queen of the Pandavas said: "Come, Draupadi, you have been won at game, give up bashfulness and see Duryodhana in the hall." Draupadi saw that it was useless to argue with the ruffian and in her anguish, ran towards the apartments of Dhritarashtra's wife. But Duhshasana sprang forward like a wolf, caught her by the hair and dragged her along by force. She pleaded her uncleanliness and her wearing one garment only, but Duhshasana heeded not her wailings and brought her by force to the assembly-hall. "Speak, sirs," said the tortured Draupadi, "am I rightly won? Had Yudhishthira, who had sold himself, the right to stake me? It is sin if those who sit in the council do not give right judgment." Nobody answered her. Bhishma only said it was a difficult and delicate question, considering the position of a wife. There she stood in vain pleading for release, with her hair caught firmly by Duhshasana, her upper half of the body uncovered. It was a sight enough to exasperate anybody, but even her husbands only hung down their heads. Bhima alone could not control his rage. "Gamblers," said he, "have female slaves, but they do not stake them even. Oh, Yudhishthira, thou hast gambled thy wife away. Sahadeva, bring fire, I will burn the hands of this shameless gambler." "How," exclaimed Arjuna, "you never said such words before; do you forget he is our elder brother? A Kshatriya cannot refuse to play when called upon by others. Do not allow your enemies to conquer you by making you go astray from the path of duty." Vikarna, the illegitimate son of Dhritarashtra, tried to save Draupadi by giving it as his opinion that she had not been properly won, but Karna told him to keep quiet where far wiser heads hesitated to decide, and he called upon Duhshasana to deprive the Pandavas and Draupadi of their clothes. The Pandavas laid aside their valuable dress and sat almost naked. But what could Draupadi do? It was a plight miserable enough to be dragged by the hair before elders and strangers, but to be deprived of clothes it was more than enough even for the courageous queen, and as Duhshasana seized her garment she could do nothing but cry and implore the Almighty. Covering her face with her hands, and stooping down she sent her fervent prayers to Hari, the protector of the weak, the Lord of the Universe, Krishna, the chief of Yogins. There was a miracle. Every garment that was taken off gave place to another. Garment after garment was taken off, but Draupadi was still covered. He who clothes the naked had come to her assistance. The princes and the people present were wonderstruck and praised Draupadi, upbraiding Duhshasana for his shameless persecution. It was a noble and awful sight, the tormentor in vain trying to expose the virtuous queen of the Pandavas. He sat down at last tired and abashed.

Such is the story of Draupadi's clothing by Krishna, and it is sung in countless Hindu homes these thousands of years, ever encouraging Hindu women to preserve in the path of virtue. It would be ruthless to dethrone this beautiful episode from its high pedestal and to subject it to the process of simplification. Those who believe in miracles will not doubt its truth. Those, however, who do not, and there were men even in that assembly who explained the event as a trick of witchcraft, may ignore it altogether. Dhritarashtra now thought that the game had gone too far and said to Draupadi: "My dear daughter, I am pleased by thy noble conduct; ask a boon of me." "Release my husbands," said she "from their bonds." "Granted," said he, "go, Yudhishthira, with thy brothers and with thy wealth, go rule thy kingdom in peace with thy cousins. For I know you are all noble and will forgive the foolishness of my sons for my sake." It seemed to be a most joyous termination to the disastrous proceeding of the day, and the brothers with their faithful wife left Hastinapura without much ceremony. But that was not to be. The old king was terrified again when his sons told him that he had let off roused serpents. If he wanted his sons to live he must call the Pandavas back and send them to live in the forest for 12 years and to live one year more *incognito* to go into exile again if discovered. They were ready to go into exile themselves if they lost the game. As fate would have it Dhritarashtra sent for the Pandavas again and unable to refuse as true Kshatriyas they played once more and lost the game and their kingdom.

CHAPTER VII.

The Twelve Years of Exile and One Year of Disappearance.

It was a bloodless triumph. The Pandavas had been humbled and their kingdom and their empire wrested from them without a blow. "To-day begins the imperial rule of the son of Dhritarashtra," cried Karna, at which the avaricious blind monarch was perhaps not a little tickled. The poor victims of Duryodhana's fraud left the city in the guise of anchorites followed by their now illustrious queen and a few servants. Hundreds went to see them off, blaming the sons of Dhritarashtra for their cruel spoliation. Vidura asked Yudhishthira to allow Kunti, the aged mother of the Pandavas, to remain with him, and as she stayed behind she gave a touching parting blessing to Draupadi. "Daughter," said she, "do not grieve in the terrible trial in thy life. Thou knowest well the duties of a wife and art gifted with a sweet temper. It is not necessary for me to tell thee how to behave towards thy husbands, for thy chastity has adorned and purified both families. Fortunate indeed are the Kurus whom thou hast not burned to ashes by thy enraged sight. Go without hesitation. A good woman never loses her temper in the hour of difficulty and thou wilt soon be blessed and happy." Draupadi with tears flowing from her eyes and with a single blood-stained garment covering her body and with her hair untied and flowing down her shoulders said "Amen," and unhesitatingly followed her husbands.

It is not necessary to follow the Pandavas in their rambles in forests, which probably adjoined the territory they had lost. They generally lived by hunting and passed their vacant time in hearing mythological stories related by the Brahmans to Yudhishthira. Two of these episodes deserve to be related here. The story of Nala and Damayanti is well-known and has been translated into many languages, both Indian and Foreign. It was related to king Yudhishthira by Brihadashwa in answer to the query whether any king before him had been deprived of his kingdom by gambling. Brihadashwa at the end of the story taught the king the art of throwing the dice in which he himself was expert. The second story, *viz.*, that of Satyavan and Savitri was related by a Rishi in answer to the question whether there was any other lady who had so saved her husband by her chastity. Both the stories, if imaginary, are lovely productions of the poetical brain, and Damayanti and Savitri are two of the most noble conceptions of female characters. The latter is particularly revered in Hindu homes, where every woman observes a fast on the 15th of Jyeshtha in her blessed memory.

During their exile the Pandavas made a pilgrimage throughout India as it was then known, visiting holy places in the company of Brahmans. They visited various places in Bengal, the Northern Sircars, on the West Coast of India as far down as Dwarsamudra, in Kathiawar, Sindh, the Punjab and the Himalayas. The geographical indentification of these places is a subject of importance which we will notice in our geographical section. Having visited the holy places and having completed the 12 years of exile they returned to Dwaitavana and resolved to pass their one year of *incognito* at the capital of Virata, the king of the Matsyas.

Directing Dhaumya, their Guru, to take their sacrificial fires to the house of Drupada and sending Indrasena and other servants with their chariots to Dwaraka, the Pandavas with their queen marched for some days on foot along the banks of the Jamna, representing themselves as the huntsmen of king Virata. As they approached the capital, which was somewhere to the south of the Jamna, they saw a big Shami tree standing near the burial ground of the town. On that tree Sahadeva deposited, at the instance of Yudhishthira, their arms. They then changed their dresses and severally went into the city. Yudhishthira, who was now expert in the art of gambling, entered the service of Virata as a Brahman courtier who played with the king at dice. Bhima, versed in the art of cooking, became master-cook and also a gladiator. Arjuna elected to be a eunuch proficient in the art of dancing, which he is said to have learnt at the court of Indra in heaven, where he had gone during the exile to learn Astravidya. He concealed the rough spots on the arm caused by constant use of the bow by wearing brass armlets and put on white bangles and let loose his hair. Thus dressed as a eunuch he entered Virata's service and taught dancing to his daughter and other girls. Nakula and Sahadeva became respectively horseman and cow-herd and passed their time accordingly. The queen of the Pandavas was the most difficult to be disguised. Strong in her virtue and possessed of courage, she dressed herself as a Sairandhri, or a servant girl, a class of which we have no idea now, and being seen wandering without employment by Sudeshna, the wife of Virata, was taken up by her. The entry of five new men and a woman into Virata's service ought to have raised suspicion, but probably they took up their duties at different times and Arjuna's disguise as a eunuch was the least expected and the least likely to be detected, for eunuchs are usually tall and bony. Thus they passed almost the whole of their period of *incognito*, when an event raised suspicion about their character. Virata had a commander-in-chief by name Kichaka, who was a Suta by caste and who had many of his castemen in his service also called Kichakas, probably that being their family name. They were all athletes and the head of them wielded very real power in Virata's kingdom. He treated himself as the brother of Virata's queen Sudheshna, though in reality she was the daughter of the King of the Kaikeyas. Seeing Draupadi one day in attendance on the queen his lust was excited, and as she rejected his amorous offers he succeeded in inducing Sudeshna to send her to his house on some pretext. Sudeshna asked Sairandhri to bring a cup of wine for her from Kichaka's house, and suspicious though she was she had to go. It is needless to say that Draupadi resisted personal violence and giving a strong back push to the villain ran to Virata's court for redress. Kichaka enraged and abashed at being thrown down pursued her, and as she stood in the royal presence seized her by the hair and kicked her. It was an indignity worse than death itself, but as Virata said nothing she cried: "Oh, the five Gandharvas who are my husbands and who see me thus treated, will they too keep silent? Heavens! this is a life which I cannot bear." Yudhishthira, Kanka by his assumed name, replied: "Go, Sairandhri, back to Sudeshna's apartment. Your husbands perhaps do not see time yet to rescue you." Draupadi went as desired, but she was not satisfied. Burning with the insult she had received, she went clandestinely to Bhima and apprised him of what had happened. She swore she would not live if Kichaka was not dead the next day. Bhima then conceived a plan to catch Kichaka in a trap. He asked her to make an appointment with him to meet at dead of night in the dancing hall which remained unoccupied by night. He would lie there in wait and would kill him when he came. The plot was well conceived and was duly carried out. The infatuated villain fell an easy prey to the representation of Draupadi, and going to the dancing hall at night was in single combat killed by the enraged Bhima. In the morning people saw the dreadful spectacle of a heap of flesh and bones literally kneaded together, in the dancing hall of Kichaka who was to be found nowhere. It was clear that Draupadi's Gandharva husbands had killed him at night. The enraged followers of Kichaka seeking to have vengeance on her caught hold of her as she stood looking from a distance and tied her to the pier of Kichaka saying they would burn the woman with her unsuccessful lover. Poor Draupadi, trials after trials were taking away her patience. Bhima was, however, there to rescue her. Hearing her cries he ran to the burial ground and attacked the Upa-Kichakas, killed some of them, while others fled away believing him to be the Gandharva husband of Draupadi. Draupadi was set free and reached home followed by Bhima. As she entered Sudeshna's apartment, she said looking at Bhima, "I bow to thee, Gandharva prince, who had rescued me from death."

The slaying of Kichaka by a Gandharva was a great event and Duryodhana's spies, who were located in every town to discover the hidden Pandavas, informed him of it. The clue was worth following. Duryodhana asked the king of the Trigartas, who had been before defeated by Kichaka, to attack king Virata on the southern side and seize his cattle, while he himself with his army would attack him on the north. The Mahabharata is precise in stating that it was on the 8th that the Trigartas attacked Virata, while Duryodhana attacked on the 9th, but strangely enough it is not stated what month it was. Virata, accompanied by the four Pandavas, went out to meet the Trigartas on the south, leaving the town in charge of his young son Uttara. When the Kaurava army seized the cattle on the north, cow-herds ran to Uttara for help. The inexperienced boy boasted that he would gladly go out to meet the Kauravas, but unfortunately he had not a good charioteer. Sairandhri suggested that Brihannada (that was the name Arjuna had assumed) could do the duty for him if his sister Uttarā would ask her teacher in dancing to do so. It was soon arranged and Arjuna took out Uttara in a chariot. The boy as soon as he saw the vast army of the Kauravas lost courage, and jumping down the chariot ran towards the town. Arjuna, however, knowing that it was time for the Pandavas to declare themselves, pursued him and catching him by the hair brought him back to the chariot. He told him he would fight for him and asked him to drive the chariot. The chariot was then taken to the Shami-tree and the bows which had been concealed by Sahadeva therein were taken down. Uncovering his own bow Arjuna said, "This is the famous Gandiva bow which I have used these 32 years and a half, and I am Arjuna." This gives us an idea of Arjuna's age at this time. The bow was given him by Agni when the Khandava forest was burned, a little after the founding of Indraprastha and the Pandava's marriage with Draupadi. If we suppose that Arjuna was at the time of his marriage about 20 years of age, it follows that they enjoyed peace and reigned in Indraprastha for 20 years. They were then deprived of their kingdom and lived in jungles about 12 years and a half. Arjuna was thus at this time about 52. If we take the ages of the five brothers as differing by one we find that the eldest Yudhishthira was 55 years old when this fight took place.

Armed with his powerful bow and driven by Uttara, Arjuna went to fight with the Kaurava army and defeated them. The generals in the Kaurava army, Bhishma and Drona, did not probably fight in earnest, nor did Duryodhana insist on this, as his object had been gained. "We have discovered Arjuna," he said to Bhishma, "before the stipulated time and the Pandavas must go into exile again. "Well," said Bhishma, "the question is a difficult one. In every five years two months are found in excess. In these thirteen years 5 months and 12 nights are in excess. The Pandavas are versed in science and might claim these to be deducted. The Pandavas have observed their faith so far and would not have come forward unless they felt justified. They do not wish to take anything unjustly, but they would not give up what they can justly claim." The evil-minded Duryodhana said nothing and the army of the Kauravas returned to Hastinapura.

It was the first lesson in war Uttara had learnt and it was under a great master. On returning home he found that his father also had returned successful, assisted as he had been by the four Pandavas. He at once informed his father who Brihannada was, and the grateful king offered to give his youthful daughter in marriage to Arjuna. Arjuna said he had taught her as a pupil and stood to her in the relation of a father. He however accepted her for his son and the marriage was celebrated with becoming festivities when Abhimanyu, Arjuna's son, came from Dwaraka accompanied by Krishna and his sister Subhadra. The aged king Drupada also came to congratulate his sons-in-law on the end of their trouble, and he and Virata now asked them to try with their assistance to regain their kingdom.

CHAPTER VIII.

PREPARATIONS FOR WAR.

YUDHISHTHIRA now encamped himself at Upaplavya, a town on the frontier of the Matsya kingdom, and began to collect an army in view of the impending struggle. Kings Drupada and Virata were already there with their available forces, and many others joined Yudhishthira in response to invitations sent by them conjointly. Duryodhana in the meanwhile was not inactive, for he was watching the movements of Yudhishthira carefully, and he too sent invitations to the princes of India to join him in opposing Yudhishthira. Krishna's aid was sought by both and he gave the first choice to Arjuna either to take him unattended and unarmed or his army of Gopas or cow-herds. Arjuna preferred the former and Duryodhana was glad to have the latter. Balarama, Krishna's brother, stood aloof in order to avoid participation in the war and decided to go on a pilgrimage. The kings mentioned by name, who elected to join the Pandavas, were; first, Yuyudhana or Satyaki, king of the Satyavatas, who were a clan of the Yadava family; second, Dhrishtaketu, king of the Chedis (he was the son of Shisupala and it seems strange that he joined the Pandavas); third, Jayatsena, son of Jarasandha (according to the strange manners of the Kshatriyas a daughter of Jarasandha married Bhima after he had slain him in combat); fourth, the king of the Pandias; fifth, Drupada, and sixth, Virata, already mentioned. All these kings brought an Akshauhini or what may be called an army corps, and each minor addition, headed by kings not named, formed one more corps, making thus 7 Akshauhinis in all on the side of the Pandavas.

On the side of Duryodhana were ranged first, Bhagadatta, king of the Northern barbarians of yellow colour; second, Bhurishrava; third, Shalya, king of the Madras (he joined the Kauravas though Nakula and Sahedeva were his sister's sons); fourth, Kritvarma, king of the Bhojas, a section of the Yadava race; fifth, Jayadratha with his brothers, king of Sindhusauviras; sixth, Sudakshina, king of the Kambojas and Yavanas; seventh, Nila, king of Mahishmati, capital of the Deccan; eighth, the two kings of Avanti; ninth, the king of the Kaikeyas with his brothers. These brought an Akshauhini each, and together with the army consisting of three Akshauhinis brought by minor kings, the total strength on the side of Duryodhana was 11 Akshauhinis. There is some mistake apparently in this calculation, for there would be thus 12 Akshauhinis.

The strength of an Akshauhini is stated in the Mahabharata as 21,870 elephants, 21,870 chariots, 65,610 horses, and 1,09,350 foot. The lowest unit is called a Patti and consists of one elephant, one chariot, three horses and five foot. Rising from the Patti the scale ends in Akshauhini* which consists of

*3 Pattis = 1 Senamukha.
3 Senamukhas = 1 Gulma.
3 Gulmas = 1 Gana.
3 Ganas = 1 Vahini.
3 Vahinis = 1 Pritana.
3 Pritanas = 1 Chamu.
3 Chamus = 1 Anikani.
10 Anikanis = 1 Akshauhini.

21,870 of this lowest unit. Calculating on this basis we find that on the Pandava side there were 1,53,090 elephants, 1,53,090 chariots, 4,59,270 horses, and 7,65,450 foot, while on the side of Duryodhana were 2,40,570 elephants, 2,40,570 chariots, 7,21,610 horses, and 12,02,850 foot. These figures do not seem to be inordinately exaggerated if we remember that in the last battle of Panipat fought on the same plain the total strength on the side of the Marhatas was 3 lacs, while opposed to them was one lac on the side of the Mahomedans. Ashoka is said to have led armies vaster than these. The number of elephants seems however incredible. It cannot stand to reason that the proportion between foot and elephants was as 5 to 1. A vast army of elephants numbering about 5 lacs would require an amount of food which almost seems unobtainable, nor does it appear probable that the jungles of India could ever have supplied such a large number, supposing of course that much of the fertile country then as now, was inhabited by men. In the Udyoga Parva, where a different definition of Akshauhini is given, the proportion between elephants and horses is 1 to 100. The commentator has not been able to explain the discrepancy, except on the supposition that the total physical strength, not the number on both the sides, was proportionate as 11 to 7.

According to rules of war both ancient and modern messages began to be exchanged counselling peace and amicable settlement. Dhritarashtra sent Sanjaya first with a message, which was more an insult than a message of peace. The crafty son-loving monarch affected deep concern for the welfare of the world and appealed to Yudhishthira's righteousness and love for humanity, saying that it was expected of his goodness that he would rather live by begging (not in his kingdom but in the country of Drupada and the Yadavas) than go to war and be the cause of a terrible destruction of human life. The reply of Yudhishthira has been finely conceived and was eloquent and full of his sentiment of love for mankind. He threw himself entirely at the mercy of Dhritarashtra, who had brought the Pandavas up from their childhood and who had himself given them a kingdom to rule. He ended by saying that he would be content with five villages even, one for each brother, but firmly added that he was prepared for both peace and war. When Sanjaya delivered the reply in council Duryodhana thought that the Pandavas were afraid of his vast army and treated the reply with contempt.

The Pandavas now on their side decided to send Shrikrishna as a messenger of peace. They expected that his high position and his power of persuasion would enable him to effect a reconciliation between the contending parties. Each of the five brothers charged Shrikrishna with a separate message, but all were for peace, though not peace at any price. Their queen however was not satisfied. With tears flowing copiously down her cheeks she showed Shrikrishna her still unbraided hair by which she had been dragged almost naked to the council hall and wondered how her husbands, how Bhima particularly, Bhima her ever ready champion, now advocated peace! Krishna comforted her by saying: "Thus shall weep the wives of thy tormentors if they do not listen to my counsel," and started in his far-resounding chariot. He passed through a prosperous country covered with cultivated fields, for it was the month of October and the country had known no war for years together under the rule of the Kauravas. Hundreds of men flocked to see the great man on the way. Bhishma and Drona and princes and people came out of Hastinapura to receive him. He drove through decorated streets full of men and women anxious to have a look at him who was believed to be an Avatara or incarnation of Vishnu. He reached the palace of Dhritarashtra, but decided to stay for the night at the house of Vidura. The two friends passed the whole night in conversation, talking on things past and present. Having bathed in the morning and performed the proper religious duties, Krishna went to the council hall where the blind monarch surrounded by his sons and councillors like Bhishma and Drona and princes assembled from all parts of India were already present anxious to hear him. The speech which the poet makes him deliver is a masterpiece and was applauded by all, but it fell flat on the ears of the infatuated Duryodhana. Dhritarashtra admitted the force of all that he said and asked him to bring his obdurate son to a sense of his duty on this momentous occasion. Krishna now addressed Duryodhana and described the iniquities of which he had been guilty, and told him that the fate of thousands of human beings trembled in the balance and would be disposed of by his word. The proud prince was incensed rather than pleased at the words of disparagement addressed to him, and rising up walked away. It was an insult which Shrikrishna could scarcely bear. "Confine, oh, Dhritarashtra," he said, "confine thy unruly son and conclude peace with the Pandavas, thus saving the Kaurava family from destruction. One man should be abandoned to save a whole family, one family to save a whole village, one village to save a whole country." While he was thus counselling the restraint of Duryodhana, he and his councillors were proposing the arrest of Krishna himself; for the Pandavas, they said, without Krishna would be like serpents deprived of their teeth. Their purpose was suspected by Satyaki, who was waiting outside the hall, and he informed Krishna of it. Vidura at the same time said to Dhritarashtra: "Thy ill-fated son wishes to arrest Krishna, the Lord of the Universe." But Krishna interposed and said: "Oh, king, allow me to seize Duryodhana and let him, if he can, seize me. If you give me permission I will nip the war in the bud." Dhritarashtra only had his son brought to him and chid him severely for his sinful and absurd design. Krishna rose up in disgust, and as he walked away Dhritarashtra said: "Oh Janardana, you have seen how my son is beyond my control. I wish the Pandavas no ill as everybody here has seen." Krishna turned towards all present and said: "You too have seen what happened to-day in the council, how the foolish Duryodhana walked away unceremoniously and how Dhritarashtra says he is powerless. Farewell, sirs, I go to Yudhishthira." With these words he went out, followed by all present, ascended the chariot which was ready under Satyaki's escort and left for Vidura's house.

Before leaving Hastinapura Krishna paid his respects to his aunt Kunti, who was at Vidura's house, and asked if she had any word to send to her sons. The message with which she charged Krishna is one of the most powerful incitements to fight. "Tell my sons," said she, "what Vidula said to her young boy who had run away from the battlefield and was lying in bed in fear. 'Arise, thou coward: thou only pleasest thy enemy and none else. He who has no courage is doomed for life. Get up and try for thy welfare. Do not think low of thyself, nor content thyself with little. It is better to put thy hand in the mouth of a serpent than die like a dog. It is better to burn fiercely for a time than merely smoke for years. Get up then and show thy prowess or die according to thy duty, for what else is thy life for?' 'Do you wish me dead,' said the boy, 'what will you do without me?' 'Foolish man,' said Vidula, 'when thou wilt see thy mother and thy wife begging thou wilt thyself think thy life a burden.' Vidula's exhortation was effective and the boy went to fight again and succeeded. Tell Yudhishthira then, nothing is more galling to me than that with sons like the Pandavas I am dependent on others for my food. Help, Krishna, my sons to the utmost of thy power."

Krishna bade her farewell and started on his return journey. Kunti, consistent with feminine wisdom, in order to weaken the strength of the Kauravas went to Karna that day and told him who he was and asked him as his mother to give up the cause of Duryodhana.

But the honourable man was firm. He upbraided her for not having disclosed her relation earlier when he might have been spared many a dishonour. Having been assisted by Duryodhana all his life, and having stood to him as a friend all along, it would be most ungrateful on his part to give him up at that critical time. "Depart, mother, as you have come," said the proud man, "I will do one thing for you, I will kill none of my brothers except Arjuna."

CHAPTER IX.

THE FIGHT.

THE armies of the contending parties marched by common consent to Kurukshetra, a vast plain to the north-west of Dehli. Duryodhana's camp, according to the Mahabharata, extended over a length of 20 miles, and it was as beautiful and commodious as Hastinapura itself. Naturally his line of front must have extended for miles together. The front of the Pandava army was not so extended, for Yudhishthira said to Arjuna. "Brihaspati has laid it down that a small force should fight in a compact body. It should take the formation of a cone." Duryodhana placed his eleven divisions under eleven generals and Bhishma was appointed the generalissimo of the Kaurava army. Arjuna too placed his seven divisions under seven generals and appointed Dhrishtadyumna as their commander-in-chief.

Having bathed and said their prayers in the early morning the fighters moved to their positions by sunrise. It was an ominous day as the sun rose dark and dim. The human mind usually believes that portents precede and accompany terrible events. Perhaps the commotion in a vast mass of human brains is communicated to the material world by that unseen link which connects the spiritual with the mental and is therefore attended by similar commotions in the sky, the heavens and the terrestrial globe. The sky was thus at that time full of dust, the sun was lightless and pale, and the ground shook under a quake of the earth. Undaunted, however, by these omens the forces took their positions, the Kauravas facing the west and the Pandavas facing the east. At the head of the Kaurava force stood Bhishma clothed in white, with a white turban on his head, a white banner waving over his chariot, to which were yoked four white horses strong and bony. Opposed to him stood Arjuna in a golden chariot, the horses of which were also white and which was driven by Shrikrishna himself.

It was an awful moment and an awful scene, well-fitted to arouse emotions of the highest order. That lacs of men, friends, brothers and relations stood face to face, ready to take one another's life, for the sordid purpose of deciding a dispute about a small kingdom, was enough to arouse a kind and sympathetic heart like that of Arjuna, and in disgust he threw down his bow refusing to kill his revered grandfather for the sake of a paltry living. He would rather beg than do the atrocious deed. Krishna is said to have then preached his famous Gita, a book of philosophy, which has always been and will always be the solace and the wonder of the thinking world. We are not concerned here with the philosophy of that book; it is enough for us to state that he succeeded in enabling Arjuna to tide over his weak moment and making him ready to fight again.

Swayed by an emotion of another kind, king Yudhishthira took off his armour and jumping down the chariot ran on foot towards the Kaurava army. His brothers not knowing what he was going to do followed him. Princes and people laughed at him, believing he was afraid to enter on the tough contest and wished to sue for peace. Yudhishthira went straight and falling at Bhishma's feet said: "We crave thy permission to fight with thee. Bless us, oh grandfather, in this contest forced upon us." The old man was pleased with his filial conduct and blessed him. Yudhishthira similarly asked for and obtained the blessing of Drona and Kripa and his uncle Shalya, and then before returning cried loudly, "Whoever wishes to join us let him come to us and fight on our side." Yuyutsu, the illegitimate son of Dhritarashtra, alone responded to his call and was hailed by the Pandavas as a representative of Dhritarashtra, who might at least survive. Yudhishthira and the four brothers having returned, the forces arranged themselves as before and then met in a terrible onset which can better be imagined than described.

The battle soon took the form of duels between opposite chiefs and between Rathis or warriors fighting from chariots. Many of these were killed and others made senseless and in that condition taken away from the battle-field. Others still had their drivers killed and their chariots strayed unguided. Some again had their horses killed and they had to dismount and fight on foot. Bhima often grappled single-handed, mace in hand, with an army of elephants and killed many of them. Arjuna and Bhishma, Drona and Dhrishtadyumna, Duryodhana and Bhima, and many others fought duels, which it would not be interesting to the reader to describe at length and which no pen but that of Vyasa can invest with interest and variety. Thus the armies fought on till it was sunset, when the leaders on both sides sounded retreat and the armies returned to their camp. It was thus from day to day. The fight in fact resembled much what the Peshawa and the Afagan armies did when they were encamped facing each other on the same plain for about a month, fighting duels from day to day wherein noted chiefs were killed or disabled. Bhishma is said to have fought on for nine days and killed 10,000 car-warriors every day. On the tenth day the Pandavas instead of allowing Arjuna to fight a duel with Bhishma selected Shikhandi, a son of Drupada, for that purpose. As Bhishma had made a vow not to fight with him, he as expected, laid down his bow, when Shikhandi assailed him in this condition. Arjuna and others from all sides shot arrows at him, which stuck into his body in numbers till at last they looked like the feathers of a porcupine, and the old man fell from his chariot. The battle was instantly stopped. Chiefs on either side assembled round the revered warrior anxious to make their last obeisance to him. The stern warrior lying on a bed of arrows exhorted Duryodhana to stay the war for his sake and give the Pandavas half the kingdom. "Let the hostility cease," said he, "with the fall of Bhishma, for Arjuna is the foremost of all the archers as a Brahmin is amongst men." The expostulation of Bhishma was, however, of no avail, and the princes dispersed to their camps after having dug a ditch round Bhishma to prevent wild beasts approaching him, for the sage warrior was not to die till the auspicious beginning of the Uttarayana (sun's turning towards the north).

By the advice of Karna, Duryodhana now appointed Drona the commander-in-chief of the Kaurava army, and he, an old man of 85, yet as vigorous as a boy, led the Kauravas to the battle-field. For two days he fought as effectively as Bhishma. On the third he posted his army in what is called the Chakravyuha or the form of a circle within a circle. Arjuna was engaged by the Samsaptakas or 7 clans who came probably from the Afagan borders and were composed of strong and powerful warriors and whom Drona had specially deputed for the purpose of drawing Arjuna away. The Pandava army, thus deprived of Arjuna, was unable to make any impression on their enemy's array. Arjuna's young son, born of Subhadra, Krishna's sister, a boy only 16 years old, proposed to enter the Kaurava army and to shatter its formation, and king Yudhishthira through mistake or chagrin allowed him to do so. He entered the Kaurava army followed by Bhima and other leaders who were, however, stopped and defeated by Jayadratha at the entrance. Abhimanyu was now alone in the midst of a vast army, but fought with courage and determination till at last he was overpowered by six warriors throwing arrows at him at the same time, contrary to the rules of war. Deprived of his bow and arrows, his horses and charioteer killed, he sprang down, mace in hand, and was engaged by Duhshasana's son. At last he dropped down and his head was instantly smashed by his opponent's mace.

Arjuna, having defeated the Samsaptakas, returned to the Pandava force which he found shattered and cheerless. His heart sank within him, as he proceeded further and found his brothers steeped in grief. "Where is my son, the darling child of Subhadra?" cried he. "I do not see him. Did he die like a brave warrior?" Yudhishthira told him what had happened and Arjuna fell down insensible. When brought round he vowed: "To-morrow will I kill Jayadratha. If I do not, may I not go to the place where my forefathers have gone. I will burn myself on a pyre if I do not kill him before sunset to-morrow." Krishna in exultation filled his conch and so too Arjuna. There was a terrible acclamation which rose to the skies and which startled the Kauravas in their sleep.

The next day the fight was stubborn. The Kauravas, having placed Jayadratha in their rear, fought stoutly and sternly and tried their utmost to prevent Arjuna from approaching him. Bhima and Arjuna performed wonders that day and Duryodhana every moment saw how he was mistaken in refusing to listen to Krishna's proposal for peace. When Jayadratha was at last killed[1] he upbraided Drona for his pusillanimity, his evident regard for Arjuna coming in the way of his fighting honestly. The old man was stung to the quick and declared that he would not terminate the fight till either he had conquered or was dead, and that to please Duryodhana he would now kill with his Astras or divine missiles all indiscriminately. (It was a rule of war that these Astras should only be used against those who knew

[1] There is no mention in the Mahabharata as is described by later poets that Jayadratha had kicked Arjuna's son and hence had increased his wrath, nor is it stated that Arjuna finding the sun setting kindled fire to die.

their use.) It was dark and the foot on both the sides lighted and held up torches, in the glare of which the arms of the combatants flashed as they closed in desperate duels. Bhima's son Ghatotkacha, a Rakshasa, wrought terrible destruction till at last he was killed by Karña by the use of a supernatural missile which he had kept for Arjuna. After some fight the armies rested by common consent for a few hours. Horses, elephants and men tired by incessant work slept on the battlefield, which presented for a time a curious aspect. The moon rose and acting upon the sea of human beings set in motion the tide of fight which surged again into tempest. In a few hours the sun rose above the horizon and the forces fought on, the old leader of the Kaurava army being the most unsparing. Thousands of men, horses and car-warriors were slain by him by the use of ordinary and supernatural missiles. The Pandavas were now advised by Krishna to use a stratagem. It was given out by Bhima, who killed an elephant by name Ashwatthama for the purpose, that Ashwatthama was dead and when Drona heard the cry his bow fell from his hand. While in this defenceless condition, Dhrishtadyumna suddenly ran up to him and cut off his head with his sword. The Kaurava army tired and harassed was ready to give way at the slightest disaster, and the death of their commander-in-chief, as in many Indian battles, was the signal for a general rout. The most undaunted warriors set their face against the field till Ashwatthama coming to know what had happened, in rage and grief made a determined stand. His efforts were, however, of no avail, and he too gave up the fight in despair and returned to the Kaurava camp.

The next day the forces of Duryodhana came out again to fight under the leadership of Karna, in whose prowess and vain promises he had lain his greatest hopes. That day the armies fought without much result, but Karna saw that Arjuna had the advantage of having a skilful charioteer. In his vanity he asked Shalya to do a similar turn to him and Shalya consented at the importunity of Duryodhana. The second day Karna started, bragging in the vainest terms, though often put down by Shalya. He sought a duel with Arjuna, and for a time the two champion archers fought an equal fight. Unfortunately one wheel of Karna's chariot sank in a ditch, and while he was extricating it Arjuna shot him with arrows in spite of his protests that it was not a fair fight. "Was it a fair proceeding," retorted Krishna, "when you asked Duhshasana to divest Draupadi of her garments?" The vain, yet honourable man submitted to his fate and laid down his life on the battle-field. The same day Bhima had his vengeance on Duhshasana. In a duel which they fought from chariots, Duhshasana was worsted and became insensible. Like an eagle suddenly stooping down from the sky and pouncing upon a serpent on the ground, Bhima sprang from his chariot and running up to Duhshasana planted his foot on his chest. Calling aloud to Karna, Duryodhana and others, he drew his scimitar, broke open Duhshasana's chest and drank his warm blood, saying, "To those who then said, she is a cow, she is a cow, I now say, you are cows, you are cows." It was a terrible and ghastly sight, an Arya drinking human blood. Nobody dared to interfere with him and many ran away in fright, believing he was a veritable Rakshasa. Such was the vengeance which Bhima and Arjuna took upon those who had tormented and insulted the noble queen of the Pandavas on the day when the disgraceful game at dice was played in Hastinapura 13 years before.

Plunged in grief Duryodhana returned to his camp. His army had nearly been destroyed and his best generals had fallen. His cause seemed almost hopeless to every man and Kripacharya thought it was his duty to address him a few words of advice. He requested him to propose peace to Yudhishthira who would, even in his ascendancy, relinquish his rights of success and give him half the kingdom as before. Every man's life was dear to him, and there was nothing dishonourable if Duryodhana now saved his life and the lives of thousands of his soldiers who were still left to him. The reply of Duryodhana was typical of a proud and honourable Aryan: "How shall I, having stood at the head of all the princes, live to enjoy a kingdom by the sufferance of Yudhishthira? I have offended the Pandavas most grievously. Shall I now go to them and ask to be pardoned? Happiness is not everlasting in this world, and the kingdom, if gained by me, will not for ever last. Everlasting is fame and for that I will even die. Moreover a Kshatriya ought not to die on a bed in his house. His death-bed is the battle-field. My grandfather Bhishma is dead and so is Drona, Karna, Jayadratha and others. How shall I live now and what pleasure shall I derive even if I get a kingdom from Yudhishthira's grace? The world will spit at me if I save my life now, having destroyed so many noble lives for me. In fine, I will fight and die on the battle-field and follow those who have already gone to Heaven." These noble and inciting words from his mouth were received with acclamations by all who were present, and the Kshatriyas resolved to fight in spite of their reverses. Shalya was appointed commander-in-chief by Duryodhana and he promised to do all he could. He strictly advised his generals not to fight duels but engage their opponent's forces generally, a caution which was not eventually heeded owing to the habits of the warriors.

Next day the forces again assembled on the battle-field in the morning. A tough battle began, the description of which in the Mahabharata strikes us as very real and may be compared with the description of modern battles. The fight in the centre, the wings, the flanks and the rear, is described with minuteness, and the general fight did not for a time resolve into duels. It was a fight which resembled much the fight between the Peshwa Sadashiva Rao and Ahamad Shaha Abdali. Shalya, like Vishwas Rao, was killed about noon. But the fight continued in spite of his death. Shakuni, who made repeated attacks with his horse on the rear of the Pandavas, was turned away by Sahadeva who was sent by Yudhishthira specially to attack him. In the afternoon the Kaurava army gave way and the men began to run away in an irrepressible tide, not towards their camp but wherever they could find safety. There was consternation in the camp itself. Most of the guardsmen fled, leaving valuable things behind, and the keepers of the women of Duryodhana's zenana could, with difficulty, find conveyance for them. They were, however, safely reached to Hastinapura, where their sudden return was the signal for general bewailing. Duryodhana, finding that nobody heeded his attempts to stay the tide of flight, left the battlefield and concealed himself in a lake. Only three warriors inquired about him, *viz.*, Ashwatthama, Kripa and Kritavarma, and Sanjaya who had seen Duryodhana, told them that he lay concealed in the lake and had sent with him word to his father Dhritarashtra. They went to the lake and Ashwatthama deeply touched bewailed his sad condition. He asked him to come out, and aided by them to fight again with the Pandavas, victorious as they were. Duryodhana however said he was tired and would wait till the next morning. He asked the three loyal men to run away and pass the night somewhere in safety. The conversation was overheard by some huntsmen of the Pandavas who were about on their work. They informed the Pandavas who, after having vainly searched for Duryodhana, had returned to their camp. Overjoyed to get the news of their life-long enemy the Pandavas set out for the lake and standing on its bank Yudhishthira called upon Duryodhana to come out and not to conceal himself like a coward.[1]

[1] The Mahabharata does not explain what Duryodhana did when he entered into water after staying it by the force of Mâyâ, nor does it tell us when and where he learnt this Mâyâ. Perhaps he concealed himself in a house surrounded by water and the access to the house was difficult and hidden.

Duryodhana replied that he was tired and would fight the next day, adding at the same time that he, alone as he was, had now no desire to rule the earth and would resign it to him. "Fool," cried Yudhishthira, "you were not ready to give even a needle-point of earth; how do you now resign the whole earth? We do not wish to take a gift from you, but will conquer it from you. Come, get out, and fighting with us either conquer us or die."

Goaded by reproaches Duryodhana came out and, single as he was, offered to fight a duel with any single person. Yudhishthira was elated with success and said, "Well, fight with any one of us and with any weapon and rule the earth if you conquer." The witless king had again begun to gamble and Krishna cried: "What have you said, Oh Yudhishthira. Do you mean to stake the whole gain of 18 days' fight on the result of a duel, or is it that Pandu's children are fated to live for ever in the forest?" Duryodhana, however, elected to fight with Bhima, his equal in mace-fight, and Bhima assured Krishna that he would conquer his adversary. The combatants, mace in hand, now prepared themselves to fight, and princes and people sat in a circle to look on. As the fight was about to begin, Balarama arrived and was hailed by both the combatants as he was their master in that art. On the combatants went, taking rounds and rounds and striking at each other with their maces, making a terrible sound of thud. Duryodhana was the lighter and the more agile of the two and often avoided the heavy blows dealt at him by Bhima. It even appeared as if the stronger of the two might fail, and Arjuna inquired anxiously of Krishna what the result would be. There was a momentary pause, the combatants resting for a while to take breath. They soon began afresh and Bhima dealt a blow which the other evaded and had a heavy blow on his chest in return. His prodigious strength alone could sustain him under it. Burning with rage and the desire for vengeance repressed for 13 years, he sprung upon his adversary and dealt a tremendous blow. Though Duryodhana jumped up to avoid it, Bhima did not stop and the blow fell full on his thighs, the bones of which were crushed to pieces. Duryodhana fell down a dying man, and Bhima going up to him kicked his head with his foot saying, "This is the reward for your insulting Draupadi." It was a terrible moment: the spectators were taken aghast. Balarama rose up exasperated at the clear disregard of the rules of fight which did not allow a blow with the mace to be dealt below the waist. Yudhishthira too was displeased at the conduct of Bhima who had dishonoured the crowned head of a king for nothing. Krishna however assuaged all and said: "Remember, Oh brother, the Kali-yuga has begun. Moreover, Bhima had vowed to break Duryodhana's thighs when he asked Draupadi to sit in his lap." He then upbraided Duryodhana for all the evil deeds he had been guilty of and for the terrible loss of life for which his obstinacy alone was responsible, and told him that he would go to hell. The proud Duryodhana was unbending even in death. He defended himself arduously. He had performed many sacrifices and had ruled the people righteously. He was sure he would go to Heaven as he had fallen on the battle-field.

He counter-accused the Pandavas for the evil practices with which they had gained their victory, the last of which, by which they had broken his thighs contrary to rules, was not the least. The Mahabharata goes on to state that at the end of this speech flowers fell on Duryodhana from Heaven and Shrikrishna and others felt abashed and confused. Perhaps upon this statement is based the idea that the original Mahabharata represented the Kauravas as having the right on their side and as having been successful in the war. Whatever may be said about its ethics there is nothing in the statement which would support the idea that the Bharata at any time represented the result of the war as anything but favourable to the Pandavas.

CHAPTER X.

THE TRIUMPH TURNED INTO A DISASTER.

THE victorious Pandavas left the wounded Duryodhana to die on the battlefield and went for rest at night to his camp. An immense spoil consisting of gold and jewels, tents and animals fell into their hands, and the survivors of 18 days' struggle eagerly possessed themselves of whatever they could lay their hands on and joyously laid themselves for rest in their new tents. They little dreamt how dearly they were soon to pay for this. The Pandavas with Draupadi and Krishna alone stayed out of the camp for the purpose of performing some religious ceremonies.

It was a strange custom with the ancient Aryans of India that they left the dead and the dying in battle unheeded on the field of battle to be devoured by birds and beasts of prey. Probably like the Aryans of Persia they believed that this was the most fitting burial to those who had the merit of dying in battle. Ashwatthama, Kripa and Kritavarma, hearing of Duryodhana's duel, came now to the battle-field and saw the great man still alive bewailing his misfortune. Aswatthama was grieved to see the master of 11 army corps in that pitiable condition and bitterly upbraided the Pandavas for their iniquities and cried for vengeance. Duryodhana, relentless even in death, was highly gratified at his loyalty and ordered Kripa to bring water and anoint him as his commander-in-chief to carry on war even after his death. Having done this and satisfied that he would be revenged, Duryodhana, as the poet says, entered into that obscurity which is the terror of all created beings.

The three left the battle-field at nightfall and rested themselves under a large banian tree for the night. Though his companions were soon asleep Ashwatthama was awake and restless, revolving diverse schemes of vengeance. He suddenly got up on seeing an owl enter into the foliage of the tree and devour crows who, blind at night, were resting there in fancied security. He took a hint from the owl and awakening his companions asked them to assist him in destroying the Pandavas in sleep. He heeded not their argument that the act was treacherous and dishonourable. Had not the Pandavas done more treacherous deeds? Had they not deceived his father and killed him when unarmed? He would go alone if they did not like to assist him. Carried away by his enthusiasm they too followed him as he went towards the Pandavas' new camp.

The two warriors stood at the entrances of the new camp with bows and arrows, while Ashwatthama, fearless and fearful, entered it clandestinely. He first entered the tent occupied by Dhrishtadyumna and as he lay asleep throttled him to death. He scarcely gave him time to cry. He next killed Shikhandi, next the five sons of the Pandavas. An uproar was raised, but guards and warriors could not understand what was going on. Ashwatthama killed men, elephants and horses, and people began to run bewildered and unarmed.

The archers at the entrance plied their bows most unerringly and unceasingly, and thousands were put to death in their defenceless condition.

When the news reached the Pandavas they ran to the camp only to find their sons, their relations, their friends murdered in cold blood. It was a terrible sight and too much even for Yudhishthira, who cried, "Thus have we, the conquerors of all, been conquered at last through our carelessness, carelessness than which nothing is more fatal." When Nakula brought Draupadi to the camp the poor woman fell down insensible at the sight of her murdered sons and brothers. Coming to her senses she cried vehemently for vengeance on Ashwatthama. "Unless he is killed," said she, "I will take no food. Bhima, you are matchless in strength; kill the destroyer of my innocent sons." Bhima, her ever ready champion, responded to her call, and with Nakula for his charioteer immediately went in pursuit of Ashwatthama. Krishna taking with him Yudhishthira and Arjuna followed him in another car. The brothers saw the Brahman bathing on the banks of the Ganges and a fight was about to begin, for he too was ready with his bow, when Krishna and Arjuna stopped it. They did not wish to kill the only son of the preceptor of the Pandavas. They called upon him to deliver over the priceless jewel on his head in token of subjugation and to depart, a hated being who had murdered innocent men and children in sleep, to be tormented by the reproaches of his own conscience. Ashwatthama did as he was desired and the five brothers went back to Draupadi and told her that Ashwatthama had been vanquished though not killed. It was enough to satisfy the noble and ever obedient queen of the Pandavas. The lucky survivors of this terrible fight could, however, ill-conceal their grief as they marched towards Hastinapura to assume the supreme sovereignty of India. It was more a funeral procession than a triumphant march.

Dhritarashtra overladen with grief and followed by Gandhari and other bereaved women of the royal family came out of Hastinapura to bathe in the Ganges and do the obsequies of the departed. Yudhishthira went to him and made his obeisance. The old monarch, a powerful man, in his rage wished to crush Bhima in his embrace, but Krishna suspected his purpose and foiled it. When Yudhishthira went towards Gandhari he saw she was about to curse him and said: "Do curse me, oh queen, the destroyer of thousands of human beings. Bereft of elders, friends and sons, there is nothing left for me to live for." Her rage was assuaged and she consoled Draupadi with the words, "Grieve not, Draupadi, look at me who have lost a hundred sons." Kunti was no doubt happy to see her sons conquer, but Draupadi asked her, "Where are thy grandsons and where is Abhimanyu? They do not run up to thee and play in thy lap as before." In fine it was a scene of lamentation and mutual condolence. The last duties performed in the Ganges, the five brothers came up preceded by their blind uncle. Yudhishthira sat down unable to enter the city. He was entirely undone and shook to see the terrible loss caused not only in his own but in every Kshatriya family. He called his brothers, wife and friends and asked their permission to retire from the world. The episode of 16 ancient kings who had preceded him and signalised their reigns by the performance of Ashwamedha sacrifices and who in spite of their greatness had after all left this world was then related to him by Krishna. Arjuna, Bhima and Draupadi asked him to remember how he had promised them in their wanderings in the forest that the period of trial would be succeeded by happiness. He was at last induced to get up and he entered the city in a triumphant procession. There were some, however, who were the friends of Duryodhana and hostile to him, and Charvaka spoke aloud as he passed: "Fie upon thee, destroyer of thy own race. It is better to die than to live like this." King Yudhishthira however by the suavity of his reply disarmed all opposition: "I bow to all. I deserve, steeped in distress as I am, I deserve to be pitied but not hissed at." There were many however who disclaimed all such sentiments and they blessed king Yudhishthira. Passing on, Yudhishthira occupied Duryodhana's palace and was there with Draupadi crowned Emperor, Krishna himself sprinkling the holy water on their head. Brahmins chanted Vedic blessings in sonorous tones and at the end praised his merits to the skies. Yudhishthira then addressed those assembled thus: "Blessed indeed are the sons of Pandu who are extolled by the Brahmanas. Know ye all that Dhritarashtra, my uncle, is adored by me. Those who wish to please me should always obey his orders." Then began in Hastinapura the benign rule of Yudhishthira, who, like Rama, made the happiness of the people his highest aim.

After a few days Yudhishthira went to the Kurukshetra again where his grand-uncle Bhishma was lying on a bed of arrows waiting for the auspicious beginning of the Uttarayana. Hundreds of Brahmin sages and princes, including Krishna, accompanied him. Having bowed to him in due form and inquired after his health, Yudhishthira asked Bhishma to teach him the duties of kings, of persons placed in difficulties and of those who had given up the world. The Shanti-parva and the Anushasana-parva, wherein are given the answers given by Bhishma to the questions put by Yudhishthira, are a mine of information regarding the state of society and of religion and philosophy as it then existed. Bhishma having answered all his questions and satisfied all his doubts dismissed him advising him to forget his grief for the past and to enjoy the fruit of the hard fought contest. The ancient sage warrior called Yudhishthira again when the favourable moment arrived and gave up his soul in peace in the contemplation of God, and his obsequies were duly performed by the survivors.

Yudhishthira now thought of performing an Ashwamedha or horse-sacrifice for his purification from sin. But where was the money to come from? He could not lay the princes of India under contribution, for they had already suffered much. He was advised by Vyasa to go to the Himalayas where untold wealth was lying from the time of the sacrifice performed by Marutta. Accordingly the brothers went on an expedition to the Himalayas where having sacrificed to God Shiva they found what they had come for.

During their absence Uttarā, Abhimanyu's wife, gave birth to a dead child. He was probably born 7 months old and had suffered in the womb owing to the shock which his mother must have received on hearing Abhimanyu's death. The last ray of hope of future progeny was thus gone and a cry of wailing came from the female apartments of the Pandavas' palace. Shrikrishna who had come there for the Ashwamedha was moved by the lamentations of Subhadra, his sister, Kunti, his father's sister, Draupadi and Uttara. He took the still-born child in his lap and swore: "As I have not spoken an untruth even in joke let this child come to life. As I have never run away from battle, as I have always held Dharma and Brahmanas dearest to me, as I have never gone to fight for the sake of quarrel alone, let this child come to life." And slowly the child began to breathe and the joy of the Bharata women knew no bounds. The child thus saved by the Yogic power of Krishna was named Parikshit.

When Parikshit was a month old the Pandavas returned from the Himalayas bearing with them immense loads of gold and jewels; they were overjoyed to hear Krishna's last act of kindness towards them and they worshipped him as their life-long benefactor. Preparations were immediately begun for the performance of the sacrifice. A horse was let loose and it roamed about the world followed by Arjuna. There were very few who could oppose the hero of the Bharata war, and the few that could, gladly tendered their submission to him. Later poets have, however, related another Mahabharata over this world-conquering tour of Arjuna and the Ashwamedha of Jaimini is an illustration of it. When the horse returned to Hastinapura, Yudhishthira gave valuable presents to commemorate his joy, and he with his queen was at once ordained for the sacrifice. The horse was slain by the Brahmanas and his entrails were according to the Shastras thrown as oblation into the sacrificial fire. The sacred smell issuing therefrom was taken by Yudhishthira and his brothers and the Brahmanas present. At the end of the sacrifice Yudhishthira said: "The Dakshinà for Ashwamedha is the earth itself. Arjuna conquered it for me and I give it to Vyasa. Let Vyasa and the Brahmanas divide it among themselves. I with my brothers and wife will retire into the forest." "Amen," said Draupadi and the Pandavas; and a thrill of amazement and admiration went over those who were present. Vyasa praised them for their generosity and goodness, but said, "You have given me the earth and I give it back to you and give me its equivalent in coin." A crore into crore gold coins were then given by Yudhishthira, and these, together with all the golden utensils made for the sacrifice were divided by the Brahmanas, who loaded with riches, left Hastinapura blessing the Pandavas for their liberality. Vyasa gave his share to Kunti, who again gave it away in charity. Thus ended the horse-sacrifice of Yudhishthira, the only bright spot in the after-life of the Pàndavas, a sacrifice in which thousands were daily feasted with rich food and drink and which in the words of the poet "gleamed with heaps of gold and jewels and was a veritable sea of wine and liquor." "It was the universal talk of praise among the inhabitants of different countries."

CHAPTER XI.

THE SEQUEL.

It is stated in the Mahabharata that the Pandavas ruled in Hastinapura for 36 years after the war, but it does not seem probable that they could have pulled on so long in the enjoyment of their fortune, saddened as it was by the death of their nearest and dearest. Dhritarashtra, who was apparently treated with respect, had in reality to suffer from the insults of the never-forgiving Bhima, and sometimes had to pass his days without food. Like a true Kshatriya he therefore resolved to retire into a forest and apprised Yudhishthira of his intention. It was a shock to the already disgusted mind of Yudhishthira. He could not persuade Dhritarashtra to give up his intention, and led by Gandhari and Kunti walking on either side and followed by Vidura and Sanjaya the blind monarch left Hastinapura amid the lamentations of the Pandavas and the people. The former implored Kunti to stay behind and enjoy the fruit of the war to which she herself had incited them. But the strong-minded lady replied, "I wanted you not to beg and therefore advised you to fight. It was not for my enjoyment, for I had enough of it in my husband's time." Thus saying she went on, not heeding their importunities or the lamentations of Draupadi. Her parting advice to her sons was most laconic and pithy: "Put faith in righteousness; have minds ever great." The departure of Dhritarashtra must have taken place a few years after the horse-sacrifice; for he could not have borne his ill-treatment for 18 years as the present Mahabharata represents. Two years after their departure came the news of their death in a jungle fire in the Himalayas, and the brothers were greatly grieved to learn the news and performed their obsequies according to due form.

Some years after this (the present Mahabharata gives the period as 15 years) came the news of the destruction of the Yadavas and the death of Shrikrishna. The Yadavas were a turbulent people addicted to drink. In revelry Satyaki once taunted Kritavarma with the atrocity of his action in the night surprise on the Pandava camp. The latter retorted and rebuked him for his dishonourable conduct in killing Bhurishrava and the two at once drew their swords. Hundreds joined the combatants and fell by each other's hand. Krishna himself took part in the fight on seeing his sons killed and slew many. At last he retired from the scene and while lying in meditation under a tree was shot by a hunter in the sole of his foot. Balarama too died a similar death, being attacked by the local tribes, who must have been emboldened by the slaughter of the Yadavas among themselves.

The news of the Yadavas fighting among themselves a war as destructive as the Mahabharata war, leaving only children and females alive in the city, caused great concern to the Pandavas, and Arjuna hastened to

Dwaraka to take care of the defenceless survivors. He was hailed by them as their deliverer, and taking them with him he started on his return journey to Hastinapura. Reaching the country of the five rivers (he probably took a circuitous route) he was attacked by barbarians armed with sticks only, their cupidity being aroused by the beauty and wealth of the women he escorted. The Mahabharata relates that Arjuna's never-failing arrows failed and he at that time even forgot the divine missiles. Although he fought bravely with his bow used as a stick, the barbarians succeeded in carrying away many women and some indeed went of their free will. Such is the testimony of the truth-loving Vyasa, who does not conceal the fact and it is a fitting commentary on the custom of keeping many women in the harem.

The death of Shrikrishna cut off the last tie which bound the Pandavas to this world and Dharma observed to Arjuna that Destiny bound all persons high or low. "Destiny! Destiny! Destiny!" cried Arjuna and the word was echoed by Bhima, Nakula and Sahadeva. The five Pandavas now resolved to leave the world and start on Mahaprasthana. The ancient Aryans of India, usually ascetic in spirit, disdained to die a wretched death at home. When the business of life was over and life was thought to be a burden, many courageous Aryans made Mahaprasthana or the great journey. It was a regular ceremony recognised by the Dharmashastras. The Pandavas placed Parikshit on the throne in Hastinapura and Vajra, Krishna's nephew, in Indraprastha. They asked Subhadra to remain behind to take care of the two young princes thus installed, they being, respectively, her grandson and nephew. Kripa was appointed Parikshit's guardian and Yuyutsu was appointed minister. Yudhishthira's parting advice to Subhadra was to "preserve in the path of Dharma or righteousness," a watchword of the great Epic. The Pandavas having sacrificed to the fire for the last time threw it into the Ganges and, followed by their wife Draupadi, started towards the north-east. They crossed the Himalayas, proceeded beyond the great desert and went onwards till at last one by one they fell down dead.

Parikshit, it has already appeared, was born about two or three months after the Mahabharata war was over and was, by the dispositions made by the Pandavas, evidently a minor at this time, probably not more than 16 years of age. How many years Parikshit ruled it does not appear; probably the supreme sovereignty of India was enjoyed by him, though his rule was undoubtedly weak. For the people called the Nagas rebelled against him. The story of Parikshit's death as related in the Mahabharata may be thus simplified. Takshaka, who was a leader of the Nagas, was the hereditary enemy of Parikshit. The Nagas had been destroyed in the Khandava forest by Arjuna and Takshaka was one of those who escaped from the conflagration. Takshaka probably founded a small kingdom in Takshashila, which was named after the Takshaka people. He appears to have fought against the Pandavas in the great war and aided Karna, for Karna is said in the Mahabharata to have used Takshaka as an arrow against Arjuna unsuccessfully. Having missed his aim Karna refused to use Takshaka again. Failing in his desire to take vengeance while Arjuna was alive Takshaka appears to have waited for his opportunity against his grandson. Parikshit having been cursed by a Rishi to be bitten by a serpent confined himself in a water palace to which no access was allowed to anybody. A Brahmin once presented fruit to Parikshit and from one of these a small worm came out which Parikshit took up in jest and said, "Let this worm bite me in order that the sage's curse may be fulfilled[1]," and verily the worm grew into Takshaka himself who bit him and then flew away in the sky. This story in the Mahabharata probably means nothing more than that Parikshit was invested in his own city Hastinapura, and was eventually assassinated by Takshaka in his own palace, to which he gained access in the dress of a Brahmin.

The minister of Parikshit made a firm stand and repulsed the attack of Takshaka, who retired to his place. Janmejaya, the young son of Parikshit, was placed on the throne of Hastinapura and grew up into a daring and resolute monarch. When he heard how his father had been murdered by Takshaka he resolved to take a signal vengeance on him. The story of Sarpasatra given in the Mahabharata Adi-parva is only a mythological transformation of the deadly war of extermination which he waged against Takshaka and his people. He attacked Takshashila and reduced it to submission. Every Naga or serpent was hunted out and sacrificed in the Sarpasatra, which was not an ordinary sacrifice pre-

[1] This account somewhat differs from the story given in the Bhagawata, where Parikshit is not represented to have jested.

scribed in the Vedic ritual but specially ordained for Janmejaya. Serpent after serpent was sacrificed or put to death and in terror Takshaka ran to Indra for shelter. A Brahmin now saved Takshaka in the person of Astika, who was born of a serpent mother and who promised to use his influence with Janmejaya to save his mother's kindred. He appeared before the king and having pleased him by his praises and his learning asked a boon of him which he granted. "Spare the lives of those serpents," said he, "who are yet alive," and the king said "Amen." Astika was ever since revered by the serpents as their saviour, and to this day whenever a Hindu sees a serpent, he cries "Astika," "Astika," and the serpent, it is believed, does no harm.

It was at the Sarpasatra that the poem composed by Vyasa is said to have been recited to Janmejaya by Vaishampayana. And this does not seem unnatural. Janmejaya would undoubtedly be anxious to know the details of the great war fought by his illustrious ancestors in which Takshaka, the enemy he now pursued, fought against them. Having heard the great poem and having finished the serpent-sacrifice or the campaign against the serpents by granting an amnesty to the survivors, Janmejaya returned (so the Mahabharata relates) from Takshashila to Hastinapura. It thus appears probable that the Bharata was first recited in Takshashila.

Janmejaya, son of Parikshit, was no doubt a powerful king known not only for his Sarpasatra or campaign against the Nagas but also for the horse-sacrifice he performed. His horse-sacrifice was, according to the

Harivamsha, where its story is given, the last that was performed in India, for horse-sacrifices thenceforth were interdicted. The descendants of Janmejaya are also given in the Harivamsha. They appear to have retained kingly power in the family for a long time till at last the Pandavas disappeared from among the ruling princes of India and were known in the days of Buddha only as a mountain tribe. The Tuars, the only Rajput tribe, who claim to be descended from the Pandavas, re-established an empire at Delhi in the 8th century A.D. under Anangapal and continued to be the foremost race of India till the beginning of the 13th century, when Prithvi Raj (who was not a Tuar but a Chavan), a relative of the last Tuar king, lost the empire of India in the famous battle of Panipat fought on the same Kurukshetra against the Mohamedan Shahabudin Ghory. The Tuars then sought refuge across the Chambal and are now to be found there under the Gwalior Raj in bare fulfilment of the prophetic blessing given by Yayati to his filial son Puru :—

> The sun may perish and the silvery moon,
> But not the line of Puru on this Earth.

APPENDIX.

NOTE I.

The Extent of the Mahabharata.

The following table will show the number of chapters and shlokas in the 18 Parvas as Sauti has given the figures in Chapter I of the Adiparva and also the number of chapters and shlokas as they are actually found in the Bombay edition of the Mahabharata.

No.	Parva.	No as recited in the Mahabharata.		No. actually found	
		Chapters	Shlokas.	Chapters	Shlokas.
1	Adi	227	8884	234	8466
2	Sabha	78	2511	81	2709
3	Vana	269	11664	315	11854
4	Virata	67	2067	72	2327
5	Udyoga	186	6698	196	6618
6	Bhishma	117	5884	122	5817
7	Drona	170	8909	202	9593
8	Karna	69	4964	96	4987
9	Shalya	59	3220	65	3608
10	Sauptic	18	870	18	810
11	Stri	27	775	27	826
12	Shanti	329	14732	366	13732
13	Anushasana	146	8000	169	7839
14	Ashwamedha	103	3320	92	2852
15	Ashramvasi	42	1506	39	1085
16	Mausal	8	320	8	287
17	Mahaprasthanik	3	320	3	109
18	Swarga	5	209	6	307
19	Khil and Harivamsha ...	....	12000	......	12580
	Total ...	1923	96836	2111	95826

From the above table it will appear, first, that the reputed extent of the Mahabharata, *viz.*, 100,000 shlokas is an approximate figure, the actual extent being, even as enumerated by Sauti, 96,826, and, secondly, that the Mahabharata, as we have it in the Bombay edition, contains 95,826 shlokas, that is to say, contains 1,010 shlokas *less* than the number declared by Sauti.

NOTE II.

THE SUBPARVAS.

The minor parvas as given by Sauti are as follows:—

1—ADIPARVA, 18.

1 Paushya legend. 2 Paulomi legend. 3 Astika legend. 4 The genealogy. 5 The birth of the Pandavas. 6 The burning of the lac house. 7 Hidimba. 8 The killing of Bakasura. 9 Meeting with Chitraratha. 10 Swayamvara of Draupadi. 11 The Marriage. 12 The coming of Vidura. 13 The attainment of a separate kingdom. 14 Arjuna's pilgrimage. 15 The abduction of Subhadra, 16 Marriage presents given by Krishna. 17 The burning of the Khandava forest. 18 The appearance of Mayasura.

2—SABHAPARVA, 9.

1 Erection of an assembly hall. 2 Counsel for the assumption of imperial dignity. 3 The destruction of Jarasandha. 4 The conquest of the four quarters. 5 The Rajasuya sacrifice. 6 The presentation of

honours. 7 The killing of Shishupala. 8 The game at dice. 9 The second Dyuta.

3—VANAPARVA, 22.

1 The killing of Kirmira. 2 The departure of Arjuna. 3 His combat with Kirata. 4 His arrival at the Indraloka. 5 The episode of Nala. 6 The pilgrimage of the Tirthas. 7 The killing of Jatasura. 8 Battle with Yaksha. 9 Battle with Nivatakavacha. 10 Meeting with the great serpent. 11 Markandeya Samasya. 12 Conversation of Draupadi and Satyabhama. 13 Cattle-lifting. 14 Deer appearing in dream before Yudhishthira. 15 Vrihidraunika. 16 The abduction of Draupadi. 17 The releasing of Jayadratha. 18 The episode of Rama. 19 Praise of the chastity of Savitri. 20 The depriving of Kundalas. 21 Araneya. 22 Aindradyumna.

4—VIRATAPARVA, 5.

1 The entry of the Pandavas into the capital of Virata. 2 The keeping up of the agreement. 3 The killing of Kichaka. 4 The capture of the cows. 5 The marriage of Uttarā.

5—UDYOGAPARVA, 11.

1 Mustering the forces. 2 The departure of Sanjaya. 3 The waking of Dhirtarashtra. 4 Sanatsujata. 5 The point of departure. 6 The departure of Shrikrishna for mediation. 7 The departure of the armies. 8 Ulukadutagamana. 9 Ratha tirtha. 10 The episode of Amba. 11 Quarrel between Bhishma and Karna.

6—BHISHMAPARVA, 5.

1 The installation of Bhishma. 2 The geography of Jambukhanda. 3 The description of its extent. 4 The Bhagawatgita. 5 The death of Bhishma.

7—DRONAPARVA, 8.

1 The installation of Drona. 2 The killing of Samsaptakas. 3 The killing of Abhimanyu. 4 Arjuna's vow. 5 The killing of Jayadratha. 6 The killing of Ghatotkacha. 7 The death of Drona. 8 The discharging of Narayanastra.

8—KARNAPARVA, 1.

9—SHALYAPARVA, 4.

1 Shalya's death. 2 Duryodhana hiding in a lake. 3 The duel. 4 Saraswata.

10—SAUPTIKAPARVA, 2.

1 Sauptika. 2 Aishika.

11—STRIPARVA, 3.

1 Giving water to the dead. 2 The lamentation of the women. 3 Shraddhaparva.

12—SHANTIPARVA, 6.

1 The duties of a king. 2 Duties in adversity. 3 Mokshaparva. 4 The checking of Charvaka. 5 Coronation of Dharmaraja. 6 The division of houses.

13—ANUSHASANAPARVA, 2.

1 Dana Dharma. 2 Bhishma's ascending to heaven.

14—ASHWAMEDHAPARVA, 2.

1 The horse-sacrifice. 2 The Anugita.

15—ASHRAMAVASIPARVA, 3.

1 Dhritarashtra's resort to the forest. 2 The sight of a son. 3 The coming of Narada.

16—MAUSALPARVA, 1.

17—MAHAPRASTHANIKAPARVA, 1.

18—SWARGAROHANAPARVA, 1.

SEQUEL, 3.

1 Hari Vamsha.
2 Vishnu Parva.
3 Bhavishya Parva.

The above will eminently serve as a table of contents. The total number of Parvas is thus 107, but by omitting some of them, attempts are made to reduce the number to 100. For instance the commentator takes 16 Sub-parvas under Vanaparva whereas we have taken them to be 22. The shlokas, we think, in the Mahabharata Chapter II, Adiparva, beginning from 42 to 84, wherein these Parvas are enumerated, cannot give less than 107 Subparvas. Thus Saraswataparva is enumerated as such in shloka 73 and yet the commentator does not count it as a Parva. It is probable that the number 100 assigned by Sauti for the Subparvas is like the round number assigned by him for the Shlokas, only an approximate one. As a matter of fact the number of Parvas in Vaishampayana's work must have been much less than 100.

NOTE III.

KUTA SHLOKAS.

Kutà or riddle shlokas are to be found throughout the Mahabharata, but principally in the first Parvas and rarely in the later Parvas. The following are some of the glaring examples:—

ADIPARVA.

1. "Nagairiva Saraswati." The last word is explained as a landscape containing a lake.

2. "Bhaganetraharam haram." Bhaga is explained as Kama or cupid; Netra as Sharira or body, Haram as Nashanam or destroyer.

3. "Kamayanamiva Striyah tyajanti." Kamayanam is explained as Kamatah yanam yasya, *i.e.*, he who wanders about at pleasure.

SABHAPARVA.

1. "Mansatalam bherim." Mansa is twelve and tala a short span, *i.e.*, a drum with 12 spans as diameter.

2. "Sangrame tarakamaye."

VANAPARVA.

1. "Tridashanabhyavarshanta danadagdha ivadrayah."

2. "Parthiva-putra-pautrah."

3. "Attashulah janapadah shiva-shulah chatushpathah: kesha-shulah striyo rajan bhavishyanti yugakhshaye."

The commentator quotes the following explanatory shloka :—

Attamannam shivo vedah Brahmanashcha chatushpathah ; Kesho bhagam samakhyatam shulam tadwikryam viduh.

Virataparva.

1. Sarvashweteva maheyi vane jata tri-hayani."

"Upatishthata Panchali vasiteva nararshabham."

2. "The well-known shloka " Nadijalamkeshvanari-ketun Nagavhayo nama Nagari-sunu ; Eshonganaveshdharah Kiriti, Jitwa vayam neshyati chadya gavah."

3. "Bindavo jatarupasya shatam yasminnipatitah, sahasrakotisanvarnah kasyaitaddhanuruttamam."

4. "Shalabhayatra sauvarnah tapaniyavibhushitah". Sahasrakoti is explained by the commentator as sahasra strong and koti the ends of a bow and sauvarna in the next shloka meaning sandal or chandana.

Udyogaparva.

1. "Ekayadwe vinishchitya trichaturbhirvasham kuru, Pancha jitwa shadwiditwa sapta hitwa sukhi bhava."

2. "Sa kritwa Pandavan satram lokam sammohayanniva, Adharmanaratan mudham dagdhumichhati te sutah." Satra is explained as Misha.

3. "Kinasha iva varnah."

Bhishmaparva.

1. "Tudanti mama gatrani maghama segawa iva."

DRONAPARVA.

1. "Natanartakagandharvaih purnakaih vardhamanakaih."

2. "Tato Bhagirathi Ganga Urvashi chabhavatpura duhitritwam gata rajnah puttratwamagamattada."

3. "Yenayatau makhamukhau dishashavihapadapah Tenashasthatumichhanti tamgatarajanishwaram."

4. "Kalasya grasato yodhan Dhrishtadyumnena mohitan."

5. Eka chakramivarkasya ratham saptarshayo hayah."

KARNAPARVA.

1. "Hamsamshugauraste sena hamsah shara ivavishan."

2. "Govardhano nama varah subhadram nama chatwaram."

3. The following is the worst example of its kind :—

"Gokarna sumukhi kriten ishuna goputrasampreshita, goshabdatmaja bhushanam suvihitam suvyaktagosuprabham, drishtwa gogatakam jahara mukutam goshabda-go-puri vai, gokarnasanamardanashcha nayaya na prapya mrityorvasham."

The word "Go" is in its different senses used here.

SHANTIPARVA.

1. "Chaturbhischa chaturbhischa dwabhyam panchabhirevacha ; huyatecha punar dwabhyam sa me Vishnuh prasidatu."

2. "Kokilasya varahasya meroh shunyasya veshmanah, Natasya bhakti-mitrasya yatshreyah tatsamacharet."

3. "Tirthanam rhidayam tirtham shuchinam rhidayam shuchih."

ASHWAMEDHAPARVA.

1. "Varanasyamupatishthat Maitreyam swairini kule."

The commentator explains Swairini as swan irayatiti, dharmaya prerayati munishrenih.

NOTE IV.

The additions subsequently made to the Bharata.

In this note we intend to give all the chapters or Adhyayas which appear to us to have been subsequently added to the Bharata of Vaishampayana by Sauti.

ADIPARVA.

1. The Paushya legend is evidently a subsequent addition as it is entirely irrelevant. It has no connection with the Mahabharata story and is only linked to it at the end. But the connection breaks off again. (Chap. 3.)

2. The Paulomi Akhyana is also irrelevant. This is introduced by the coming of Suta to Shaunaka and begins as if nothing had been written before this. The story is an Arabian Night story and is intended to glorify the obedience of Kshatriyas to Rishis. (Chap. 4—12.)

3. The Astika story is repeated. All these Akhysnas are inferior in composition. The shlokas beginning

with "Tadagata jvalitam" describing the battle of gods and the demons are irrelevant and not very poetical. Similarly, the description of the sea when Vinata and Kadru came to it and crossed it is out of place. The Stutis of Indra and Surya are of the hackneyed kind identifying everything with the God praised. The way in which these stories are knit together is in the fashion of the Arabian Nights being usually introduced by a casual mention or haphazard question. (Chap. 13—58.)

4. The story of Kashyapa and Takshaka and of Parikshita's death is repeated.

5. The Amshavatara is a subsequent addition; each actor in the great scene is described as the incarnation of some god or demon. The details here given sometimes contradict what is stated in other places. (Chap. 59—66.)

6. The story of Yayati is repeated. (Chap. 75—85.)

7. The "Uttara Yayati Akhyana" is a subsequent addition and is unconnected with the principal story. It is also given in long metred shlokas. It gives the tenets of Hinduism, however, in short pithy language and is well worth studying. (Chap. 86—93.)

8. The chapter in prose giving the genealogy of the Pandavas is followed by another in verse. The latter is an interpolation as has been shown in the book. (Chap. 95.)

9. The story of "Ani Mandavya" is repeated. (Chap. 107—108.)

10. Vyasa's appearance on the scene and advice to Dhritarashtra to throw away his son is a subsequent addition for reasons mentioned in the body of the book. (Chap. 158.)

11. The names of Dhritarashtra's sons are twice repeated. (Chap. 115—116.)

12. The story of Pandu killing a deer is twice repeated, the shloka "Sarvabhutahite kale" being also repeated. (Chap. 118.)

13. The appearance of gods in the heavens and the Akashavani vouchsafed every time is probably a subsequent addition. The poet finds an opportunity to display his power of enumerating the gods and other divine beings.

14. The birth of Kripa and Drona is wonderful. Rishis emitting semen at the sight of beautiful Apsaras and the semen germinating in some way into men is the usual Pauranic account of great men's birth. (Chap. 130.)

15. The stories of Hidimba and Baka are like children's stories and very probably interpolations. (Chap. 154—166.)

16. The story of Drona and Drupada is repeated again.

17. The story of the king of Gandharvas playing in the Ganges water is an interpolation. Here we have the usual artifice adopted, *viz.*, the gift of divine sight to Arjuna.

18. The Gandharva and Arjuna sitting together after a fight and telling stories of Tapati and Vishwamitra is almost comical and the Akhyanas are added here uncongenially. (Chap. 172—175.)

19. The stories of Vasishtha and Kalmashapada and Bhargava and Aurva are quite out of place. They are tedious and almost trying in the march of the proper story. (Chap. 177—184.)

20. The story which Vyasa relates to Drupada explaining why Draupadi can have many husbands is a subsequent addition as has already been shown.

(Chap. 198—199.)

21. The story of Sundopsaunda is a typical Pauranic story. Asuras inflated by the obtainment of a boon from Shiva destroy themselves. (Chap. 211—214.)

Sabhaparva.

1. The Rishis mentioned in the Yudhishthira Sabha are repeated in the Brahma Sabha. (Chap. 11—12.)

2. The story of the game at dice is repeated. The repetition is explained by Janemejaya asking for greater details of the event. The same shlokas are often used.

(Chap. 73—80.)

Vanaparva.

1. The Tirthas are repeated as already shown.

(Chap. 82—84.)

2. The story of Agastya and his drinking up the sea is perhaps out of place here. (Chap. 103—104.)

3. The conversation in Chapters 132—134 is philosophical and tough for the commentator even. The whole conversation consists of shlokas which may be looked upon as riddles and the commentator has himself composed Stragdhara shlokas to explain the meaning of each.

4. The story of Yavakrita is not charming and the language also not good. (Chap. 135—138.)

5. The story of Varaha incarnation is entirely unconnected as no Tirtha suggests it. The language also is not good. (Chap. 142.)

6. The story of Bhima meeting Hanuman is not probable as Bhima already knows who Maruti is. It is perhaps a later addition. (Chap. 147—150.)

7. Maruti's description of the four Yugas and again of the Ashramas is entirely irrelevant.

8. The story of Bhima trespassing into Gandhamadana and killing Mani at Draupadi's request is a repetition. Kubera chides Bhima in a manner which should lead him again to fight rather than submit. Bhima is represented as acting foolishly and here, too submissively.

(Chap. 146, 160, 161, 162.)

9. Markandeya's coming and telling different stories is probably a later addition. The object is the extolling of Brahmanas and the glorification of Krishna as an incarnation of the supreme deity. We find here verse mixed with prose which seems to have been

introduced here as a variety. The story of Shyena and Kapota is repeated. (Chap. 182—231.)

10. The story of Kumara's birth is different from that given in the Puranas and in Kalidasa's well-known poem called Kumarsambhava. He is represented here as the son of Agni. (Chap. 222—225.)

11. The conversation between Satyabhama and Draupadi is puerile. The picture which the latter draws of a good wife is that of a humble woman who washes the household pots and clothes, and not that of a queen.

(Chap. 231—234.)

12. The story of Duryodhana being bound and carried away by Chitraratha is a later addition. It seems absurd for Indra to wish for Duryodhana's being taken to him bodily. (Chap. 241.)

13. The subsequent story of Duryodhana sitting for Prayopaveshana, *i.e.*, fasting until death, and his being carried by a Kritya to Patala is an absurdity.

(Chap. 250.)

14. Durvasa's going to the Pandavas to tease is again an absurd story subsequently added. Durvasa cannot be supposed to have descended so low.

(Chap. 261.)

15. The story of Karna's Kundalas being taken away by Indra is repeated here. The story has already been told in the Adiparva, and Janmejaya ought to have known it, yet Janmejaya asks questions here as if he knew nothing. Again, if Karna is deprived of his

Kundalas at this time and from thence called Karna, he should not have been called Karna up to this time which we do not find to be the case. (Chap. 299—309.)

16. The Yakshaparashna episode, as has already been stated in the body, is an interpolation. (Chap. 312.)

VIRATAPARVA.

1. Uttara's running away from the chariot and then becoming an exceptional charioteer and a poet, has already been commentated upon. The Virataparva is the most poetical of all the parvas and the story is well diversified, but there are very few separate Akhyanas in it. (Chap. 42—43—45.)

UDYOGA-PARVA.

1. Shalya's promise has been commentated on in the body of the book as absurd and unpoetical. (Chap. 7.)

2. The story of Shakrajaya is a repetition of Vrittravadha related in the Vanaparva. Nahusha's story is also related in short. (Chap.8—9.)

3. Vidura Niti is a good teaching for all times. But it is somewhat out of place. (Chap. 32—39.)

4. The dialogue between Sanatsujata and Dhritarashtra is too philosophical to suit a character like that of Dhritarashtra. (Chap. 40—45.)

5. The Chapter 48 of 109 shlokas is a tiresome addition. Arjuna did not say anything of the kind to Sanjaya, who yet gives a lengthy message as from him in long metre.

6. The whole dialogue is unskilfully extended. The question by Yudhishthira is out of place.

7. Chapter 59 is clearly a later addition. Sanjaya is not before represented as speaking to Krishna and Arjuna in private. Moreover Krishna was not young then but old as stated in the Sabhaparva.

8. The Rishis Kanva and Narada coming to exhort Duryodhana and relating several stories is an improbable interruption of the natural march of the story.

9. Krishna's taking Karna with him and offering him empire after disclosing to him who he is, is unnatural as it lowers Krishna's character, and how could Sanjaya have known it when both Krishna and Karna kept it a secret?

10. Unfavourable astronomical conjunctions and other bad omens are here added as has already been stated.

11. The message sent with Uluka is unnecessarily lengthy. The message actually delivered by him is, however, good and pointed. The replies given by the several Pandavas are again twice repeated.

(Chap. 159—163.)

BHISHMAPARVA.

1. The appearance of Vyasa and his proposal to give eyes to Dhritarashtra is a subsequent interpolation. "The Bhumi-khanda" is also an interpolation as already observed. (Chap. 11—12.)

2. The praise of Devi appears also to be a later addition.

3. Chapters 65 and 66 are probably subsequent additions in praise of Krishna and the support of the Vaishnava sect, for after all this it is strange that Duryodhana remains firm.

4. In the beginning of Chapter 69 we have "Duryodhana Uvacha" which is probably a mistake for "Bhishma Uvacha."

5. Krishna's giving up the reins of Arjuna's chariot horses and running to kill Bhishma—a fine scene—is twice repeated. (Chap. 107—108.) The proposal to go and ask Bhishma how he should be killed, is also an absurdity already commented upon.

DRONAPARVA.

1. This Parva seems to be more elaborate than the preceding ones and seems to have been entirely recast. The similes follow one upon another as in the modern Purana. There is a long metred shloka (Shardulavikridita) at the end of Chapter 7 which is strange. Again Dhritarashtra says that Drona had studied the four Vedas and the fifth Akhyana, by which is meant usually the Bharata. How could he when Bharata had no existence in his days? Dronaparva is also more imaginary and mythical.

2. The long-metred shlokas in this Parva are diversified. The consolation of Subhadra and her lamentations are probably interpolations, the same shlokas as those uttered by Arjuna being used. (Chap. 77.)

3. So also is the chapter where Arjuna in a dream is taken to Shiva. (Chap. 80.)

4. Similarly the next chapter where the splendour of Dharma's royal functions of bathing, etc., are described. This is clearly shown by the fact that the next chapter begins with Dhritarashtra's question "what happened the next day." The next day had already dawned and Sanjaya had already told Dhritarashtra what Arjuna and Krishna had done. (Chap. 84.)

5. Dhritarashtra says "I do not hear to-day the same noise as usual in the houses of Saindhava." This shows that he was in camp or even if he was in Gajapura it is not every day that Sanjaya told him of the battle. It was only after Drona's death that he came to him and told him what had happened. (Chap. 85.)

6. The story of the fight between Satyaki and Bhurishrava is a later addition. Probably Bhima was in Satyaki's chariot. When did he leave it? The spectacle of two men dischariotíng each other is strange. So also their fighting like gladiators with naked arms in the midst of a raging battle; and what was Arjuna doing all the while? (Chap. 142—143.)

7. There is much of pure hyperbole in the account of Bhima's throwing away the chariot of Drona bodily 7 times with his hands.

8. The chapters relating the second fight between Drona and Ghototkacha is a later addition probably. They revile each other and yet Drona does not refer to his previous defeat by him. Secondly, Ghatotkacha

brought with him one Akshaunhini but he is not said in the beginning to have brought one with him. Thirdly, he is said to have destroyed 8 and subsequently 7 Akshauhinis, which is impossible.

9. The appearence of Vyasa at the end of Chapter 184 is unnecessary and useless.

10. The commentator admits at the end that the number of shlokas in this Parva is more than the one given by Sauti and attributes the fact to the mistake of writers. How can the number increase by the fault of writers? Interpolation is clearly admitted here.

KARNAPARVA.

1. The story of Shankar killing Tripura is repeated and very closely to the previous story which appears at the end of the Drona Parva. (Chap. 34.)

2. The absurdity of Duryodhana telling the story, for stories should properly be told by elders, is explained in the poem "I heard this story when a Brahman related it to my father."

3. Repetition and lengthening of scenes is a bad feature of Ṡauti's composition.

4. In the midst of bragging, Karna remembers two curses pronounced upon him by a Brahmin which is absurd. These are probably later additions.

5. The mixed fight described in Chapters 55 to 63 is a tiresome extension of the same story. The speech of Yudhishthira is also very long.

6. The scene between Yudhishthira and Arjuna, the former upbraiding the latter for nothing, and saying "accursed be thy bow" and the latter drawing his sword to kill him, is inconsistent with the character of both and not at all appropriate and pleasing. The solution given by Krishna is also not worthy of his teaching. (Chap. 68.)

SHALYAPARVA.

1. Shalya's fighting with Bhima is impossible as he had already been removed from battle senseless. (Chap. 16.)

2. Sanjaya's telling Dhritarashtra about Yuyutsu coming to Vidura and staying with him for the night, is absurd. How could Sanjaya know it? Vidura was with Dhritarashtra. In one place Sanjaya says "Dhrishtadyumna seized Sanjaya" which ought to have been "me" if Sanjaya himself is the relator. (Chap. 29.)

GADAPARVA.

1. Janmejaya interrupting Vaishampayana at the very time when the centre of interest is reached and the fight between Bhima and Duryodhana about to begin, for a description of the Saraswati river and the pilgrimage of Balarama has already been commented upon. (Chap. 35.)

2. Krishna's coming to comfort Dhritarashtra and Gandhari is rather strange. It does not fit in with the story which is still told by Sanjaya. The last sentence of Sanjaya is "He went to Gandhari whose sons were

killed." But Gandhari was not there, she having been sent away. Sanjaya could not also have seen this as his extraordinary vision had gone. Moreover, when Krishna appears he sees Dhritarashtra and Gandhari together. (Chap. 63.)

3. The story of the chariot of Arjuna burning to ashes as soon as Krishna got down is absurd. For Krishna got down from the chariot every evening, and where is the beauty of describing Arjuna as destroying the Brahmastra of Drona and Karna by counter Astras?

SAUPTIKAPARVA.

1. The propitiation of Shiva by Ashwatthama is a later addition meant to add to the horror and success of his crime. (Chap. 7.)

2. Ashwatthama's going back to Duryodhana to inform him of the slaughter of the innocent is also inconsistent, for the latter had already died at the end of the previous Parva. (Chap. 9.)

3. The greatness of Mahadeva and Linga worship come in at the end of this Parva unnecessarily.

STRIPARVA.

1. Repetition of scenes and even of the same shlokas is exemplified in the comforting speeches of Vidura and Sanjaya. (Chap. 2—4.)

2. Vyasa giving sight to Gandhari is a repetition of the same idea. Her description of the battlefield is unpoetical and has already been commented upon. (Chap. 16—17.)

3. The curse of Gandhari to Krishna is an unnecessary foretelling of future events as has already been shown. (Chap. 25.)

SHANTIPARVA.

1. Subhadra appears here to have been in Dwaraka while before she was in the camp and was comforted for Abhimanyu's death.

2. There is a deal of repetition in Vyasa's and Arjuna's speeches. The story of the 16 kings is here repeated. (Chap. 22, 27, 28, 29.)

3. The story of Syamantapanchaka and Parasharama destroying Kshatriyas is repeated here. It has already appeared in the Adiparva.

4. Yudhishthira asking his brothers about Dharma, Artha and Kama, and Bhima urging him to have beautiful women, etc., is thoroughly out of point and out of place.

5. The stories of Bodhya and Kashyapa and Indra are probably later additions. (Chap. 178.)

6. Chapters 190 and 192 are in prose and in the fashion of modern Shastras. They appear to be later additions.

7. The praise of Vishnu, the creation of the world and the working of the three Gunas are constantly touched.

8. The conversation of Bali and Indra is repeated. Repetition in this Mokshaparva is almost irksome. In Chapter 248, Gunas and the elements are repeated, a

thing which has been done perhaps for the 5th time. Shlokas from the Gita frequently recur. (Chap. 223, 224, 227.)

9. The story of Death or Mrityu is repeated. (Chap. 255, 257.)

10. The story of Jajali and Tuladhara is a subsequent addition probably in support of Ahimsa. (Chap. 260, 263.)

ANUSHASANAPARVA.

1. The story of Vishwamitra becoming a Brahmin is unnecessarily repeated here. (Chap. 3—4.)

2. The Upamanyu Akhyana and the thousand names of Shiva is a subsequent addition as has already been noted. (Chap. 17.)

3. The next chapter is an abrupt breaking off on the evil disposition of women.

4. The power and sanctity of Brahmins is reiterated. The story of Shibi is told once more. That these stories should come under Dana-dharma is strange. Probably in the original Anushasanaparva the only subject touched was gifts. (Chap. 32—33.)

5. The story of Vishwamitra becoming a Brahmin is told once more in a fanciful form.

6. The origin of gold is told and the story of Kartikeya's birth is repeated. Popularly mercury is believed to have been born of Shiva's semen and not gold. (Chap. 84, 85, 86.)

7. "I wish to know this Oh Brahman in detail." (Chapter 95.) Here the word Brahman as addressed to Bhishma is strange.

8. The Uma-Maheshwar Samvada is an interpolation and an absurdity. The hackneyed questions are asked again. A Brahman here is said to have been born and good conduct can only make one a Brahmana in the next life. (Chap. 140—148.)

9. Krishna and Durvasa is the same story as Chyavana and Kaushika related before. (Chap. 159—160.)

10. In the morning prayer, Chapter 166, the rivers are repeated again.

ASHWAMEDHAPARVA.

1. There is a repetition of Dharmaraja's grief and his consolation by Vyasa and Krishna. (Chap. 1—15.)

2. It seems that the story of Uttanka and the Mani has already been told in the Adiparva in another form. (Chap. 53—58.)

3. How could the Earth console Subhadra at the death of Abhimanyu. ?

4. The chapter in which a nakula despises the horse sacrifice of Yudhishthira is a later addition in defence of Ahimsa. (Chap. 90.)

5. The story that the nakula was under a curse is still a later addition and inconsistent with the previous chapter. (Chap. 92.)

ASHRAMAVASIPARVA.

1. Dhritarashtra's advice to Yudhishthira how to govern the kingdom is quite inconsistent with the character of both. (Chap. 6—7.)

2. Narada said confidently that the gods were talking among themselves that he (Dhritarashtra) would go to Kuber Loka. This is rather strange and probably an interpolation. (Chap. 38—39.)

3. The description given of the Pandavas and their wives is quite out of place as Dhritarashtra could not have realised it, for he is not only blind but is now a hermit.

4. The appearance of the dead is an old idea—as old as the Bharata. Janmejaya being shown his father is, however, a clear later addition.

MAHAPRASTHANIKAPARVA.

1. The story of the Pandavas going west, south and east and seeing Dwaraka submerged is absurd. They could not have walked so long, and the Mahaprasthana, according to the Dharmashastra, is only towards the north-east. (*See* Boudhayana's Dharmashastra.) (Chap. 1, 2, 3.)

SWARGAROHANAPARVA.

1. The soul of each actor in this Epic is said to have returned after death to the deity from which it sprang. This is probably a later idea.

2. The last chapter giving the description of the Parvas is clearly an interpolation. Vaishampayana has gone away and Janmejaya has returned to Gajapura and Suta has told Shaunka the merit of reading Bharata. It is strange that Janmejaya should come again to ask Vaishampayana to give a detail of the Parvas. Moreover, we have here a mention of the Ramayana, the 18 Parvas and the worship of Hari and Krishna.

NOTE V.

Explanation of the double positions of planets mentioned in the Mahabharata.

The actual positions of the planets on or about the several dates assigned to the Mahabharata war are as follows. I am indebted for these calculations to Professor Apte of the Lashkar College:—

KARTIKA VADYA AMAVASYA.

(Friday) Shake −3180.

Planets.	Degrees.	Nakshatras.
Sun	234° 56′ 2″ ...	Jyeshtha.
Mercury	225° 32′ 52″ ...	Anuradha or Jyeshtha
Venus	218° 26′ 34″ ...	Anuradha.
Mars	258° 39′ 43″ ...	Purvashadha or Uttarashada.
Jupiter	350° 22′ 22″ ...	Revati.
Saturn	314° 55′ 8″ ...	Shatataraka.
Rahu	235° 18′ 29″ ...	Jyeshtha.

Solar eclipse must have occurred. Lunar eclipse cannot have happened on the preceding full-moon day.

2. Kartika Vadya Amavasya.

(Saturday) Shake −2567.

Planets.		Degrees.		Nakshatras.
Sun ...	...	233° 41′ 20″	...	Jyeshtha
Mercury...	...	241° 22′ 58″	...	Mula.
Venus ...	...	278° 43′ 30″	...	Uttara or Shravana or Dhanishtha.
Mars ...	...	238° 22′ 4″	...	Jyeshtha or Mula.
Jupiter (retro)	...	237° 28′ 22″	...	Jyeshtha or Mula.
Saturn (retro)	...	254° 31′ 51″	...	Purvashadha or Uttarashadha
Rahu ...	...	219° 56′ 31″	...	Anuradha.

Solar eclipse highly probable. Lunar eclipse did occur on the preceding full-moon day.

3. Kartika Vadya Amavasya.

(Friday) Shake −2527.

Planets.		Degrees.		Nakshatras.
Sun ...	...	212° 4′ 58″	...	Vishakha or Anuradha.
Mercury...	...	214° 27′ 57″	...	Anuradha.
Venus ...	...	255° 58′ 26″	...	Purva or Uttarashadha.
Mars ...	...	298° 26′ 9″	...	Dhanishtha or Shatataraka.
Jupiter ...	...	13° 42′ 10″	...	Bharani.
Saturn ...	...	24° 15′ 3″	...	Bharani or Krittika.
Rahu ...	...	162° 43′ 58″	...	Hasta.

No solar eclipse nor lunar possible.

4. KARTIKA VADYA 10.

(Sunday) Shake −1271.

(Corresponding to 31st October 1194 B.C.)

(Date assigned by Mr. Ayyar.)

Planets.		Degrees.		Nakshatras.
Sun ...	...	231° 13′ 37″	...	Jyeshtha or Mula.
Mercury. .	...	246° 41′ 49″	...	Mula or Purva.
Venus ...	...	233° 18′ 57″	...	Jyeshtha or Mula.
Mars ...	...	251° 35′ 24″	...	Mula.
Jupiter ...	...	322° 52′ 12″	...	Purvabhadrapada.
Saturn ...	...	253° 54′ 27″	...	Purvashadha.
Rahu ...	...	88° 5′ 25″	...	Punarvasu.

No solar eclipse nor lunar possible.

The happening of a solar eclipse immediately before the war is a fact which is probably true and cannot be supposed to have been invented later. From the above we gather further corroboration of the generally accepted date. The date given by Garga's dictum, according to my interpretation, *viz.*, 2,566 years before the Shaka era, seems also a probable date. The other dates appear from the above to be improbable.

This is, however, a diagression. Comparing these positions with the positions mentioned in the Mahabharata we cannot but doubt that the latter are fictitious. Moreover, the chapter in the Udyoga Parva, wherein Krishna is represented as trying to wean Karna from the cause of Duryodhana, we have already shown to be an interpolation. So is the chapter in the beginning of the Bhishma Parva, wherein Vyasa tries to induce Dhritarashtra to intervene and stop the impending fight, and offers to give him supernatural vision if he wishes to see it. In these two chapters, these astronomical references are chiefly to be found, and we have no doubt that they were introduced by Sauti to swell the list of evil omens that were then happening. They, however, deserve to be carefully considered even supposing that they are later additions; for, they must be supposed to have been cleverly introduced and not recklessly. We will, therefore, try in this note to see how far these apparently contradictory statements can be reconciled and what the commentator has to say in this connection.

Before going on to the subject, it will be necessary to place before the reader the Sarvatobhadra Chakra which the commentator sometimes refers to in explanation. The Chakra is quoted from the astronomical work of Narapati called Narapativijaya and frequently referred to on questions relating to war. We give below the barest outline of it as it will suffice our purpose.

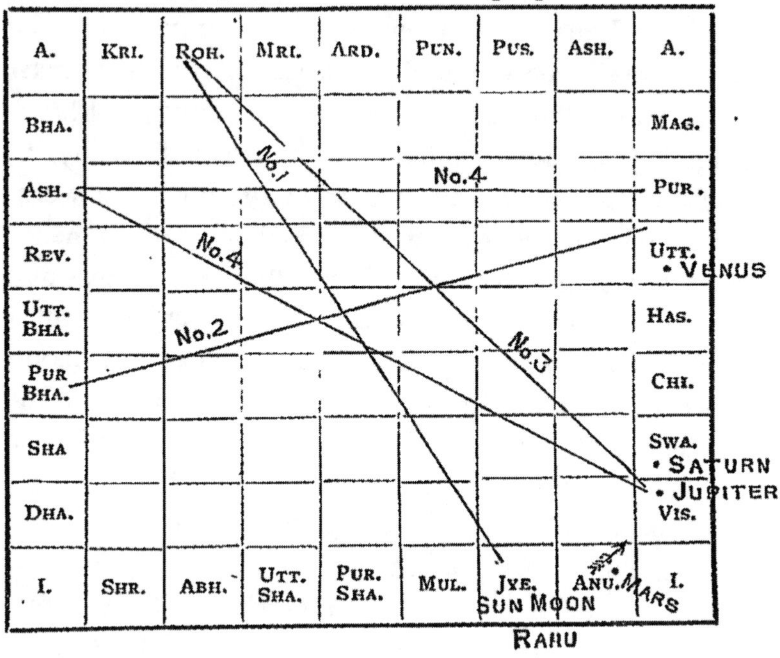

The Chakra places seven Nakshatras in each side of a square, beginning with the Krittikas, and puts 4 letters in the corners simply for convenience. The planet from any of these Nakshatras have Vedhas in different directions and chiefly in three. When the planet is retrograde it has a Vedha backwards, when forward in motion, it looks ahead and all have a Vedha in the cross line. There are other supplementary Vedhas which we need not refer to here.

Now it is admitted by all that Krishna started on his mission of peace in the month of Kartika when the moon was in the Revati Nakshatra. "Kaumude masi Revatyam sharadante himagame" Udyoga Parva, Chapter 82. He must have taken two or three days to reach Hastinapura and two days to finish his work. When he left, he said to Karna "Seven days hence there will be Amavaśya and let fight begin on that day as it is presided over by Shakra." Now the commentator thinks that on the Amavasya day the moon was expected to be in Jyeshtha, and Mr. Ayyar, Author of the "Date of the Mahabharata" lately published, also thinks the same. The Jyeshtha Nakshatra is presided over by Indra. Duryodhana moved his army on the Pushya Nakshatra, *i.e.*, the next day or immediately after Krishna left. From Pushya to Jyeshtha the moon could not apparently have passed in 7 days, and Mr. Ayyar surmises that 7 days is a mistake for 10. But he forgets that that fortnight is said to have consisted of 13 days only, and the moon's motion must have been very rapid.

Karna, in his conversation with Krishna, makes the following observations (Chapter 142, Udyoga-Parva):—"The Nakshatra of Prajapati (Rohini) is oppressed by the evil planet Saturn. Mars turning back from Jyeshtha seeks Anuradha. Particularly the planet oppresses Chitra. The condition of the moon is reversed and Rahu is approaching the sun." As the evil dark half is usually believed to begin from Vadya 5th, this was spoken by Karna, presumably on or after the 5th of the dark half of Kartika. Pushya or Punarvasu might easily fall on that day.

Hereafter the armies of the contending parties move to, and encamp in, Kurukshetra. Convenient camps are pitched for different divisions, camps said to be more commodious and full of comforts than Hastinapura itself. This must have taken several days. Meanwhile Vyasa visits Dhritarashtra and makes an attempt at inducing the old man to stop the coming fight, but in vain. Vyasa mentions the following evil omens:—"There is a comet standing over Pushya. Among the Maghas Mars is retrograde and Jupiter is in Shravana. Saturn is standing over the Bhaga Nakshatra (Purva) and Venus shines over the Purvabhadrapada. The white planet stands over Jyeshtha. Both the sun and the moon oppress Rohini. The evil planet stands between Chitra and Swati. The red planet, making counter-retrograde from retrograde, stands over Shravana, the Rashi of Bramhâ. Jupiter and Saturn stand near Vishakha. The sun and the moon were eclipsed together on the 13th. I have seen Amavasya on the 14th day, but never on the 13th."—(Chapter 2, Bhishma-Parva.)

From this it appears clear that the actual fighting commenced after the Amavasya or new moon and not before, as Mr. Ayyar thinks on the basis of Bhishma's remark on the day of his death, that he had been lying on his bed of spikes for 58 days. It also appears certain that the sun, the moon, and Rahu were together near Jyeshtha, as there could not have been an eclipse of the sun otherwise. We can thus understand Karna, speaking before Amavasya, when he remarks that Rahu is approaching the sun. Again, Vyasa's statement that both the sun and the moon oppress Rohini, is explicable as from Jyeshtha by cross Vedha the sun and the moon have an evil influence on Rohini. (*See* red line No. 1.) Venus may be supposed to be in Uttara, from there shining over Purva Bhadrapada. (*See* cross red line No. 2.) Karna's statement "particularly the planet oppresses Chitra," and Vyasa's statement "the evil planet stands between Chitra and Swati," must both be taken to refer to a comet or some evil fictitious star.

Having fixed the sun and the moon and Rahu, we will go on to locate Mars, Jupiter and Saturn. Different statements regarding these have given rise to different interpretations. Mars is said to be retrograde in Magha, and counter-retrograde in Shravana, while from Karna's speech it appears that it was going back from Jyeshtha towards Anuradha. Modaka takes only two of these, *viz.*, Magha and Anuradha, and thinks that Magha is only a Sâyana name for Anuradha, but he entirely ignores the third position mentioned, *viz.*, in Shravana. The commentator believes that Mars was really in

Magha and stood over Shravana by Vedha according to Sarvato-bhadra Chakra. But here the commentator forgets that Karna has located Mars between Jyeshtha and Anuradha. We think the proper explanation is that Mars being retrograde was going from Anuradha towards Vishakha when Vyasa spoke. Being retrograde his Vedha from Anuradha goes to Magha, being the first Nakshatra in each side. Thereafter he turns counter-retrograde and from near Vishakha his Vedha goes forward to Shravana in the same way. In this manner can the three statements be best reconciled. Jupiter is said to be in Shravana and also near Vishakha. The commentator thinks that Jupiter was in reality in Shravana and his Vedha went from there to Vishakha, being the last Nakshatra in each side. Similarly Saturn, he thinks, was in reality in Purva (or Bhaga Nakshatra) and his Vedha went from there to Vishakha also; for this he refers to a second Chakra called the Shatapada Chakra. It is unnecessary to enter into what he propounds. We think that the word "Samîpastha" is very clear and that both Jupiter and Saturn are represented by Souti as near Vishakha. Modak has not tried to explain the positions of Saturn at all. There is a third statement about Saturn in Karna's speech, where he is said to oppress Rohini. These statements may thus be explained. From Vishakha the Vedha of Jupiter goes to Shravana in the forward line. The Vedha of Saturn from near Swati (and whence he advanced towards Vishakha at the time of Vyasa's speech) goes towards Rohini as shown by red line No. 3. As for the Purva or Bhaga Nakshatra which is said to be oppressed by Saturn, we can take the Vedha from between Swati and Vishakha to Ashwini by the transverse line and from thence direct to Purva. *See* red line No. 4.)

It will appear that these different Vedhas or oppressions are nearly the same as astrological drishtis, as these are understood in modern astrology which recognises 4 kinds of drishtis, *viz* :—(1) full or semicircular, *i.e.*, at a distance of 14 Nakshatras; (2) three-fourths or triangular, *i.e.*, at a distance of 9 or 18 Nakashatras; (3) one-half, *i.e.*, quadrilateral, *i.e.*, at a distance of 7 or 21 Nakshatras; and (4) one-fourth or hexagonal, *i.e.*, at a distance of 4 or 16 or 24 Nakshatras taking figures approximately. Saturn's Vedha of Rohini and Purva is at distances of 16 and 24 Nakshatras respectively.

It may be added that the intention of Sauti in giving these Vedhas was to show that the Nakshatras appertaining to life or creation, *viz.*, Rohini and Shravana, presided over by Brahma or the Creator, and Purva presided over by Bhaga and Magha presided over by the Pitris, were oppressed by the evil sights of planets. We may also take it that Mars going retrograde and approaching Saturn, was then, as now, believed to be the sign of an impending destructive war. The Boer war was immediately preceded by a similar conjunction.

We may here incidentally discuss the question when the actual fighting took place and here comes the famous shloka "That day the moon was in the 'region' of Magha and the seven planets appeared in the sky shining." Mr. Ayyar relies on this, coupled with the declaration of Bhishma at the time of his death, *viz.*, that he had been lying on his bed of spikes for 58 days, and believes that the moon was in the beginning of the fight in Magha, *i.e.*, the fight began five days before the Kartika Amavasya. But this gives us only two days after the armies were moved on Pushya for the pitching of camps, etc., which seems quite insufficient and is inconsistent with all other statements in the Mahabharata, especially that of Balarama who arrived on the last day of the fight and said "It is forty-two days since I started. I left in Pushya and have returned in Shravana." The commentator interprets Maghavishaya as the region of the deity of Magha, *i.e.*, of the Pitris (souls of ancestors) which are believed to reside in the moon, which is again the deity of Mriga, and hence thinks that the moon was in Mriga and thus reconciles this fact with Balarama's arrival in Shravana (which is 18 Nakshatras from Mriga) on the 18th day of the fight. The Bharata Sawitri, a work which the commentator quotes, believes that the moon was in Bharani which is presided over by the God of Death and is thus allied with Maghavishaya. But the commentator objects that from Bharani to Shravana there are 21 Nakshatras which the moon could not go over in 18 days. But it is admitted by him that the fight began on the 13th of Mrigashirsha bright half, that Bhishma fell on the 8th of the dark half, that the terrible fight at night when Drona was commander-in-chief happened on the 12th, and thus the description in the Mahabharata that the moon rose about 3 a.m. on that night is consistent and that Duryodhana was killed on the Amavasya of Mrigashirsha. Now we have shown before that on the Amavasya of Kartika when there was an eclipse of the sun the moon was in Jyeshtha. From Jyeshtha to Mriga there are 15 Nakshatras which the moon would ordinarily require 14 days to go over. The statement of Bhishma that he lay on his bed for 58 days is reconciled by the commentator by a pun upon the word Ashtapanchashat which ordinarily means 58 but is made to mean 42 by deducting the same from one hundred. From Mrigashirsha 8th of the dark half when Bhishma fell wounded to Magha 5th bright half when he is supposed to have died we count 42 days only but not 58 and the commentator has succeeded in transforming 58 into 42. But he has forgotten to notice another remark in the Anushasanaparva where Yudhishthira is said to have stayed 50 nights in Hastinapura after the end of the war and then gone to see Bhishma, as he was to die when Uttarayana would commence. On our part we think it is impossible to reconcile these statements unless we change the reading of some of them as Ayyar has done or reject some as interpolations. It is safest and involves the least change to reject the last two statements in the Anushasanaparva so that all the rest are reconciled and to hold that the moon was either in Mriga or Bharani on the first day of the fight. Mr. Modak, who takes that the moon was in real Magha and Sayana Mriga, is not troubled by the discrepancy in the number of days intervening between Bhishma's fall and death.

The second half of the shloka is equally a riddle like the first. All the seven planets can never shine in the sky at the same time, for when the sun shines the rest must be invisible. But granting that this was then observed as an abnormal event it must at least be shown that the 7 planets were then above the horizon. If we believe along with the commentator that Jupiter was in Shravana he could not then have been above the horizon but was below it and similarly with Venus. This clearly shows that the positions we have assigned to the planets are those which Sauti assigned them. From Amavasya to the 14th the sun might be supposed to have travelled from Jyestha to Mula and the moon from thence to Mriga. When the sun rose, therefore, on that day he rose along with Mercury, Mars and Jupiter, and Saturn near him, Venus a little above and the nearly full-moon near the west. It is possible that they might all have been visible and shining if the sun was cut by clouds as we are told in the next shloka.

NOTE VI.

Janmejaya's Brahmahatya.

What Janmejaya's Brahmahatya was is a mystery and it is feared must remain so for ever. We have consulted many men versed in the Vedic and Puranic lore but none has been able to find out any legend or any story in any Purana in this connection. The story given in Adiparva, Chapter II, seems to have been abruptly cut off. It would be interesting to give its substance here. Janmejaya Parikshita was performing a sacrifice when some dogs entered the sacrificial ground and were beaten and turned out. Sarama, their mother, cursed Janmejaya and his brothers for ill-treating the dogs for no fault of theirs, and said that an unforeseen evil would befall them. The king in fright went to a Rishi, named Shrutashrava, who gave his son Somashrava as Upadhyaya to the king and told him that he would be able to purify him from all his Papakrityas except Mahadevakritya. The son, however, had one fault, *viz.*, that he would give to any one any boon asked of him. The king took him on that condition and having told his brothers to do whatever he ordered went to Takshashila which he conquered. Here the story ends and unfortunately (this is the only place in the Mahabharata where the context is so hopelessly cut off) no mention is further made as to what unforeseen evil befell the brothers and what help Somashrava gave to the king and what boon was asked of him and by whom. This Somashrava has not even been mentioned among the Rishis who were present at the Sarpa Satra performed by Janmejaya. Possibly Sauti purposely left out the remaining story and changed it into the subsequent story of an Ashwamedha performed by Janmejaya, given later on in Harivamsha where Indra is said to have ravished the queen of Janmejaya when she was made to lie down with the slaughtered sacrificial horse as is laid down by the ritual of Ashwamedha. Janmejaya thereon in anger banished the Brahmanas engaged in the sacrifice and turned out the queen from his house. He was, however, induced to accept her back on intercession by the Rishis but declared that none should thenceforth perform an Ashwamedha. This prohibition is still observed by most Kshatriyas.